DICK HEBDIGE

SUBCULTURE
THE MEANING OF STYLE

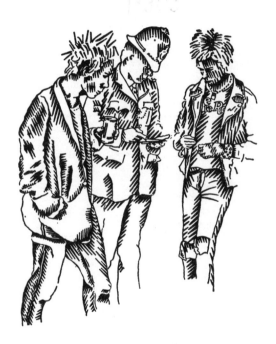

ROUTLEDGE

LONDON AND NEW YORK

EG13183

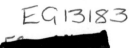

First published in 1979 by Methuen & Co. Ltd
Reprinted ten times
Reprinted 1987

Reprinted 1988, 1989, 1991, 1992, 1993, 1994
by Routledge
11 New Fetter Lane, London EC4P 4EE
29 West 35th Street, New York, NY 10001

Printed in England by Clays Ltd, St Ives plc

British Library Cataloguing-in-Publication Data available

Library of Congress Cataloging-in-Publication Data available

ISBN 0-415-03949-5

CONTENTS

Part Two: A reading

GENERAL EDITOR'S PREFACE

I T is easy to see that we are living in a time of rapid and radical social change. It is much less easy to grasp the fact that such change will inevitably affect the nature of those disciplines that both reflect our society and help to shape it.

Yet this is nowhere more apparent than in the central field of what may, in general terms, be called literary studies. Here, among large numbers of students at all levels of education, the erosion of the assumptions and presuppositions that support the literary disciplines in their conventional form has proved fundamental. Modes and categories inherited from the past no longer seem to fit the reality experienced by a new generation.

New Accents is intended as a positive response to the initiative offered by such a situation. Each volume in the series will seek to encourage rather than resist the process of change, to stretch rather than reinforce the boundaries that currently define literature and its academic study.

Some important areas of interest immediately present themselves. In various parts of the world, new methods of analysis have been developed whose conclusions reveal the limitations of the Anglo-American outlook we inherit. New concepts of literary forms and modes have been proposed; new notions of the nature of literature itself, and of how it communicates are current; new views of literature's role in relation to society flourish. *New Accents* will aim to expound and comment upon the most notable of these.

In the broad field of the study of human communication, more and more emphasis has been placed upon the nature and function of the new electronic media. *New Accents* will try to identify and discuss the challenge these offer to our traditional modes of critical response.

The same interest in communication suggests that the series should also concern itself with those wider anthropological and sociological areas of investigation which have begun to involve scrutiny of the nature of art itself and of its relation to our whole way of life. And this will ultimately require attention to be focused on some of those activities which in our society have hitherto been excluded from the prestigious realms of Culture.

Finally, as its title suggests, one aspect of *New Accents* will be firmly located in contemporary approaches to language, and a continuing concern of the series will be to examine the extent to which relevant branches of linguistic studies can illuminate specific literary areas. The volumes with this particular interest will nevertheless presume no prior technical knowledge on the part of their readers, and will aim to rehearse the linguistics appropriate to the matter in hand, rather than to embark on general theoretical matters.

Each volume in the series will attempt an objective exposition of significant developments in its field up to the present as well as an account of its author's own views of the matter. Each will culminate in an informative bibliography as a guide to further study. And while each will be primarily concerned with matters relevant to its own specific interests, we can hope that a kind of conversation will be heard to develop between them: one whose accents may perhaps suggest the distinctive discourse of the future.

TERENCE HAWKES

ACKNOWLEDGEMENTS

MANY people have assisted in different ways in the writing of this book. I should like in particular to thank Jessica Pickard and Stuart Hall for generously giving up valuable time to read and comment upon the manuscript. Thanks also to the staff and students of the University of Birmingham Centre for Contemporary Cultural Studies, and to Geoff Hurd of Wolverhampton Polytechnic for keeping me in touch with the relevant debates. I should also like to thank Mrs Erica Pickard for devoting so much time and skill to the preparation of this manuscript. Finally, thanks to Duffy, Mike, Don and Bridie for living underneath the Law and outside the categories for so many years.

'smelling of garlic, sweat and oil, but ... strong in their moral assurance' subject Genet to a tirade of hostile innuendo. The author joins in the laughter too ('though painfully') but later, in his cell, 'the image of the tube of vaseline never left me'.

> I was sure that this puny and most humble object would hold its own against them; by its mere presence it would be able to exasperate all the police in the world; it would draw down upon itself contempt, hatred, white and dumb rages. (Genet, 1967)

I have chosen to begin with these extracts from Genet because he more than most has explored in both his life and his art the subversive implications of style. I shall be returning again and again to Genet's major themes: the status and meaning of revolt, the idea of style as a form of Refusal, the elevation of crime into art (even though, in our case, the 'crimes' are only broken codes). Like Genet, we are interested in subculture – in the expressive forms and rituals of those subordinate groups – the teddy boys and mods and rockers, the skinheads and the punks – who are alternately dismissed, denounced and canonized; treated at different times as threats to public order and as harmless buffoons. Like Genet also, we are intrigued by the most mundane objects – a safety pin, a pointed shoe, a motor cycle – which, none the less, like the tube of vaseline, take on a symbolic dimension, becoming a form of stigmata, tokens of a self-imposed exile. Finally, like Genet, we must seek to recreate the dialectic between action and reaction which renders these objects meaningful. For, just as the conflict between Genet's 'unnatural' sexuality and the policemen's 'legitimate' outrage can be encapsulated in a single object, so the tensions between dominant and subordinate groups can be found reflected in the surfaces of subculture – in the styles made up of mundane objects which have a double meaning. On the one hand, they warn the 'straight' world in advance of a sinister presence – the presence of difference – and draw down upon themselves vague suspicions, uneasy laughter, 'white and dumb rages'. On the other hand, for those who erect them into icons, who use them as words or as curses, these objects become signs of forbidden identity, sources of value. Recalling his humiliation at the hands of the police, Genet finds consolation in the tube of vaseline. It becomes a symbol of his 'triumph' – 'I would indeed rather have shed blood than repudiate that silly object' (Genet, 1967).

The meaning of subculture is, then, always in dispute, and style is the area in which the opposing definitions clash with most dramatic force. Much of the available space in this book will therefore be taken up with a description of the process whereby objects are made to mean and mean again as 'style' in subculture. As in Genet's novels, this process begins with a crime against the natural order, though in this case the deviation may seem slight indeed – the cultivation of a quiff, the acquisition of a scooter or a record or a certain type of suit. But it ends in the construction of a style, in a gesture of defiance or contempt, in a smile or a sneer. It signals a Refusal. I would like to think that this Refusal is worth making, that these gestures have a meaning, that the smiles and the sneers have some subversive value, even if, in the final analysis, they are, like Genet's gangster pin-ups, just the darker side of sets of regulations, just so much graffiti on a prison wall.

Even so, graffiti can make fascinating reading. They draw attention to themselves. They are an expression both of impotence and a kind of power – the power to disfigure (Norman Mailer calls graffiti – 'Your presence on their Presence . . . hanging your alias on their scene' (Mailer, 1974)). In this book I shall attempt to decipher the graffiti, to tease out the meanings embedded in the various post-war youth styles. But before we can proceed to individual

ONE

From culture to hegemony

Culture

> Culture: cultivation, tending, in Christian authors, wor-
> ship; the action or practice of cultivating the soil; tillage,
> husbandry; the cultivation or rearing of certain animals
> (e.g. fish); the artificial development of microscopic
> organisms, organisms so produced; the cultivating or
> development (of the mind, faculties, manners), improve-
> ment or refinement by education and training; the condi-
> tion of being trained or refined; the intellectual side of
> civilization; the prosecution or special attention or study
> of any subject or pursuit. (*Oxford English Dictionary*)

CULTURE is a notoriously ambiguous concept as the
above definition demonstrates. Refracted through
centuries of usage, the word has acquired a number
of quite different, often contradictory, meanings. Even as a
scientific term, it refers both to a process (artificial development of microscopic organisms) and a product (organisms
so produced). More specifically, since the end of the
eighteenth century, it has been used by English intellectuals

and literary figures to focus critical attention on a whole range of controversial issues. The 'quality of life', the effects in human terms of mechanization, the division of labour and the creation of a mass society have all been discussed within the larger confines of what Raymond Williams has called the 'Culture and Society' debate (Williams, 1961). It was through this tradition of dissent and criticism that the dream of the 'organic society' – of society as an integrated, meaningful whole – was largely kept alive. The dream had two basic trajectories. One led back to the past and to the feudal ideal of a hierarchically ordered community. Here, culture assumed an almost sacred function. Its 'harmonious perfection' (Arnold, 1868) was posited against the Wasteland of contemporary life.

The other trajectory, less heavily supported, led towards the future, to a socialist Utopia where the distinction between labour and leisure was to be annulled. Two basic definitions of culture emerged from this tradition, though these were by no means necessarily congruent with the two trajectories outlined above. The first – the one which is probably most familiar to the reader – was essentially classical and conservative. It represented culture as a standard of aesthetic excellence: 'the best that has been thought and said in the world' (Arnold, 1868), and it derived from an appreciation of 'classic' aesthetic form (opera, ballet, drama, literature, art). The second, traced back by Williams to Herder and the eighteenth century (Williams, 1976), was rooted in anthropology. Here the term 'culture' referred to a

... particular way of life which expresses certain meanings and values not only in art and learning, but also in institutions and ordinary behaviour. The analysis of culture, from such a definition, is the clarification of the meanings and values implicit and explicit in a particular way of life, a particular culture. (Williams, 1965)

This definition obviously had a much broader range. It encompassed, in T. S. Eliot's words,

> ... all the characteristic activities and interests of a people. Derby Day, Henley Regatta, Cowes, the 12th of August, a cup final, the dog races, the pin table, the dartboard, Wensleydale cheese, boiled cabbage cut into sections, beetroot in vinegar, 19th Century Gothic churches, the music of Elgar. . . . (Eliot, 1948)

As Williams noted, such a definition could only be supported if a new theoretical initiative was taken. The theory of culture now involved the 'study of relationships between elements in a whole way of life' (Williams, 1965). The emphasis shifted from immutable to historical criteria, from fixity to transformation:

> ... an emphasis [which] from studying particular meanings and values seeks not so much to compare these, as a way of establishing a scale, but by studying their modes of change to discover certain general causes or 'trends' by which social and cultural developments as a whole can be better understood. (Williams, 1965)

Williams was, then, proposing an altogether broader formulation of the relationships between culture and society, one which through the analysis of 'particular meanings and values' sought to uncover the concealed fundamentals of history; the 'general causes' and broad social 'trends' which lie behind the manifest appearances of an 'everyday life'.

In the early years, when it was being established in the Universities, Cultural Studies sat rather uncomfortably on the fence between these two conflicting definitions – culture as a standard of excellence, culture as a 'whole way of life' – unable to determine which represented the most fruitful line of enquiry. Richard Hoggart and Raymond Williams portrayed working-class culture sympathetically in wistful accounts of pre-scholarship boyhoods (Leeds for Hoggart (1958), a Welsh mining village for Williams (1960)) but their work displayed a strong bias towards literature and literacy[1] and an equally strong moral tone. Hoggart deplored the way in which the traditional working-class community – a community of tried and tested values despite the dour landscape in which it had been set – was being undermined and replaced by a 'Candy Floss World' of thrills and cheap fiction which was somehow bland *and* sleazy. Williams tentatively endorsed the new mass communications but was concerned to establish aesthetic and moral criteria for distinguishing the worthwhile products from the 'trash'; the jazz – 'a real musical form' – and the football – 'a wonderful game' – from the 'rape novel, the Sunday strip paper and the latest Tin Pan drool' (Williams, 1965). In 1966 Hoggart laid down the basic premises upon which Cultural Studies were based:

> First, without appreciating good literature, no one will really understand the nature of society, second, literary critical analysis can be applied to certain social phenomena other than 'academically respectable' literature (for example, the popular arts, mass communications) so as to illuminate their meanings for individuals and their societies. (Hoggart, 1966)

The implicit assumption that it still required a literary sensibility to 'read' society with the requisite subtlety, and that the two ideas of culture could be ultimately reconciled was also, paradoxically, to inform the early work of the French writer, Roland Barthes, though here it found validation in a method – semiotics – a way of reading signs (Hawkes, 1977).

Barthes: Myths and signs

Using models derived from the work of the Swiss linguist

Ferdinand de Saussure[2] Barthes sought to expose the *arbitrary* nature of cultural phenomena, to uncover the latent meanings of an everyday life which, to all intents and purposes, was 'perfectly natural'. Unlike Hoggart, Barthes was not concerned with distinguishing the good from the bad in modern mass culture, but rather with showing how *all* the apparently spontaneous forms and rituals of contemporary bourgeois societies are subject to a systematic distortion, liable at any moment to be dehistoricized, 'naturalized', converted into myth:

> The whole of France is steeped in this anonymous ideology: our press, our films, our theatre, our pulp literature, our rituals, our Justice, our diplomacy, our conversations, our remarks about the weather, a murder trial, a touching wedding, the cooking we dream of, the garments we wear, everything in everyday life is dependent on the representation which the bourgeoisie *has and makes us have* of the relations between men and the world. (Barthes, 1972)

Like Eliot, Barthes' notion of culture extends beyond the library, the opera-house and the theatre to encompass the whole of everyday life. But this everyday life is for Barthes overlaid with a significance which is at once more insidious and more systematically organized. Starting from the premise that 'myth is a type of speech', Barthes set out in *Mythologies* to examine the normally hidden set of rules, codes and conventions through which meanings particular to specific social groups (i.e. those in power) are rendered universal and 'given' for the whole of society. He found in phenomena as disparate as a wrestling match, a writer on holiday, a tourist-guide book, the same artificial nature, the same ideological core. Each had been exposed to the same prevailing rhetoric (the rhetoric of common sense) and turned into myth, into a mere element in a 'second-order semiological system' (Barthes, 1972). (Barthes uses the example of a photograph in *Paris-Match* of a Negro soldier saluting the French flag, which has a first and second order connotation: (1) a gesture of loyalty, but also (2) 'France is a great empire, and all her sons, without colour discrimination, faithfully serve under her flag'.)

Barthes' application of a method rooted in linguistics to other systems of discourse outside language (fashion, film, food, etc.) opened up completely new possibilities for contemporary cultural studies. It was hoped that the invisible seam between language, experience and reality could be located and prised open through a semiotic analysis of this kind: that the gulf between the alienated intellectual and the 'real' world could be rendered meaningful and, miraculously, at the same time, be made to disappear. Moreover, under Barthes' direction, semiotics promised nothing less than the reconciliation of the two conflicting definitions of culture upon which Cultural Studies was so ambiguously posited – a marriage of moral conviction (in this case, Barthes' Marxist beliefs) and popular themes: the study of a society's total way of life.

This is not to say that semiotics was easily assimilable within the Cultural Studies project. Though Barthes shared the literary preoccupations of Hoggart and Williams, his work introduced a new Marxist 'problematic'[3] which was alien to the British tradition of concerned and largely untheorized 'social commentary'. As a result, the old debate seemed suddenly limited. In E. P. Thompson's words it appeared to reflect the parochial concerns of a group of 'gentlemen amateurs'. Thompson sought to replace Williams' definition of the theory of culture as 'a theory of relations between elements in a whole way of life' with his own more rigorously Marxist formulation: 'the study of relationships in a whole way of *conflict*'. A more analytical framework was required; a new vocabulary had to be learned. As part of this process of theorization, the word 'ideology' came to acquire a much wider range of meanings than had previously been the case. We have seen how Barthes found an 'anonymous ideology' penetrating every possible level of social life, inscribed in the most mundane of rituals, framing the most casual social encounters. But how can ideology be 'anonymous', and how can it assume such a broad significance? Before we attempt any reading of subcultural style, we must first define the term 'ideology' more precisely.

Ideology: A lived *relation*

In the *German Ideology*, Marx shows how the basis of the capitalist economic structure (surplus value, neatly defined by Godelier as 'Profit . . . is unpaid work' (Godelier, 1970)) is hidden from the consciousness of the agents of production. The failure to see through appearances to the real relations which underlie them does not occur as the direct result of some kind of masking operation consciously carried out by individuals, social groups or institutions. On the contrary, ideology by definition thrives *beneath* consciousness. It is here, at the level of 'normal common sense', that ideological frames of reference are most firmly sedimented and most effective, because it is here that their ideological nature is most effectively concealed. As Stuart Hall puts it:

It is precisely its 'spontaneous' quality, its transparency, its 'naturalness', its refusal to be made to examine the premises on which it is founded, its resistance to change or to correction, its effect of instant recognition, and the closed circle in which it moves which makes common sense, at one and the same time, 'spontaneous', ideological and *unconscious*. You cannot learn, through common sense, *how things are*: you can only discover *where they fit* into the existing scheme of things. In this way, its very taken-for-grantedness is what establishes it as a medium in which its own premises and presuppositions are being rendered *invisible* by its apparent transparency. (Hall, 1977)

Since ideology saturates everyday discourse in the form of common sense, it cannot be bracketed off from everyday life as a self-contained set of 'political opinions' or 'biased views'. Neither can it be reduced to the abstract dimensions of a 'world view' or used in the crude Marxist sense to designate 'false consciousness'. Instead, as Louis Althusser has pointed out:

> ... ideology has very little to do with 'consciousness'. ... It is profoundly *unconscious*. ... Ideology is indeed a system of representation, but in the majority of cases these representations have nothing to do with 'consciousness': they are usually images and occasionally concepts, but it is above all as *structures* that they impose on the vast majority of men, not via their 'consciousness'. They are perceived-accepted-suffered cultural objects and they act functionally on men via a process that escapes them. (Althusser, 1969)

Although Althusser is here referring to structures like the family, cultural and political institutions, etc., we can illustrate the point quite simply by taking as our example a physical structure. Most modern institutes of education, despite the apparent neutrality of the materials from which they are constructed (red brick, white tile, etc.) carry within themselves implicit ideological assumptions which are literally structured into the architecture itself. The categorization of knowledge into arts and sciences is reproduced in the faculty system which houses different disciplines in different buildings, and most colleges maintain the traditional divisions by devoting a separate floor to each subject. Moreover, the hierarchical relationship between teacher and taught is inscribed in the very lay-out of the lecture theatre where the seating arrangements – benches rising in tiers before a raised lectern – dictate the flow of information and serve to 'naturalize' professorial authority. Thus, a whole range of decisions about what is and what is not possible within education have been made, however unconsciously, before the content of individual courses is even decided.

These decisions help to set the limits not only on what is taught but on *how* it is taught. Here the buildings literally *reproduce* in concrete terms prevailing (ideological) notions about what education *is* and it is through this process that the educational structure, which can, of course, be altered, is placed beyond question and appears to us as a 'given' (i.e. as immutable). In this case, the frames of our thinking have been translated into actual bricks and mortar.

Social relations and processes are then appropriated by individuals only through the forms in which they are represented to those individuals. These forms are, as we have seen, by no means transparent. They are shrouded in a 'common sense' which simultaneously validates and mystifies them. It is precisely these 'perceived-accepted-suffered cultural objects' which semiotics sets out to 'interrogate' and decipher. All aspects of culture possess a semiotic value, and the most taken-for-granted phenomena can function as signs: as elements in communication systems governed by semantic rules and codes which are not themselves directly apprehended in experience. These signs are, then, as opaque as the social relations which produce them and which they re-present. In other words, there is an ideological dimension to every signification:

> A sign does not simply exist as part of reality – it reflects and refracts another reality. Therefore it may distort that reality or be true to it, or may perceive it from a special point of view, and so forth. Every sign is subject to the criteria of ideological evaluation. . . . The domain of ideology coincides with the domain of signs. They equate with one another. Whenever a sign is present, ideology is present too. Everything ideological possesses a semiotic value. (Volosinov, 1973)

To uncover the ideological dimension of signs we must

first try to disentangle the codes through which meaning is organized. 'Connotative' codes are particularly important. As Stuart Hall has argued, they '. . . cover the face of social life and render it classifiable, intelligible, meaningful' (Hall, 1977). He goes on to describe these codes as 'maps of meaning' which are of necessity the product of selection. They cut across a range of potential meanings, making certain meanings available and ruling others out of court. We tend to live inside these maps as surely as we live in the 'real' world: they 'think' us as much as we 'think' them, and this in itself is quite 'natural'. All human societies *reproduce* themselves in this way through a process of 'naturalization'. It is through this process – a kind of inevitable reflex of all social life – that *particular* sets of social relations, *particular* ways of organizing the world appear to us as if they were universal and timeless. This is what Althusser (1971) means when he says that 'ideology has no history' and that ideology in this general sense will always be an 'essential element of every social formation' (Althusser and Balibar, 1968).

However, in highly complex societies like ours, which function through a finely graded system of divided (i.e. specialized) labour, the crucial question has to do with which specific ideologies, representing the interests of which specific groups and classes will prevail at any given moment, in any given situation. To deal with this question, we must first consider how power is distributed in our society. That is, we must ask which groups and classes have how much say in defining, ordering and classifying out the social world. For instance, if we pause to reflect for a moment, it should be obvious that access to the means by which ideas are disseminated in our society (i.e. principally the mass media) is *not* the same for all classes. Some groups have more say, more opportunity to make the rules, to organize meaning, while others are less favourably placed, have less power to produce and impose their definitions of the world on the world.

Thus, when we come to look beneath the level of 'ideology-in-general' at the way in which specific ideologies work, how some gain dominance and others remain marginal, we can see that in advanced Western democracies the ideological field is by no means neutral. To return to the 'connotative' codes to which Stuart Hall refers we can see that these 'maps of meaning' are charged with a potentially explosive significance because they are traced and re-traced along the lines laid down by the *dominant* discourses about reality, the *dominant* ideologies. They thus tend to represent, in however obscure and contradictory a fashion, the interests of the *dominant* groups in society.

To understand this point we should refer to Marx:

> The ideas of the ruling class are in every epoch the ruling ideas, i.e. the class which is the ruling *material* force of society is at the same time its ruling *intellectual* force. The class which has the means of material production at its disposal, has control at the same time over the means of mental production, so that generally speaking, the ideas of those who lack the means of mental production are subject to it. The ruling ideas are nothing more than the ideal expression of the dominant material relationships grasped as ideas; hence of the relationships which make the one class the ruling class, therefore the ideas of its dominance. (Marx and Engels, 1970)

This is the basis of Antonio Gramsci's theory of *hegemony* which provides the most adequate account of how dominance is sustained in advanced capitalist societies.

Hegemony: The moving equilibrium

'Society cannot share a common communication system so long as it is split into warring classes' (Brecht, *A Short Organum for the Theatre*).

The term hegemony refers to a situation in which a provisional alliance of certain social groups can exert 'total social authority' over other subordinate groups, not simply by coercion or by the direct imposition of ruling ideas, but by 'winning and shaping consent so that the power of the dominant classes appears both legitimate and natural' (Hall, 1977). Hegemony can only be maintained so long as the dominant classes 'succeed in framing all competing definitions within their range' (Hall, 1977), so that subordinate groups are, if not controlled; then at least contained within an ideological space which does not seem at all 'ideological': which appears instead to be permanent and 'natural', to lie outside history, to be beyond particular interests (see *Social Trends*, no. 6, 1975).

This is how, according to Barthes, 'mythology' performs its vital function of naturalization and normalization and it is in his book *Mythologies* that Barthes demonstrates most forcefully the full extension of these normalized forms and meanings. However, Gramsci adds the important proviso that hegemonic power, precisely *because* it requires the consent of the dominated majority, can never be permanently exercised by the same alliance of 'class fractions'. As has been pointed out, 'Hegemony ... is not universal and "given" to the continuing rule of a particular class. It has to be won, reproduced, sustained. Hegemony is, as Gramsci said, a "moving equilibrium" containing relations of forces favourable or unfavourable to this or that tendency' (Hall *et al.*, 1976a).

In the same way, forms cannot be permanently normalized. They can always be deconstructed, demystified, by a 'mythologist' like Barthes. Moreover commodities can be symbolically 'repossessed' in everyday life, and endowed with implicitly oppositional meanings, by the very groups who originally produced them. The symbiosis in which ideology and social order, production and reproduction, are linked is then neither fixed nor guaranteed. It can be prised open. The consensus can be fractured, challenged, overruled, and resistance to the groups in dominance cannot always be lightly dismissed or automatically incorporated. Although, as Lefebvre has written, we live in a society where '... objects in practice become signs and signs objects and a second nature takes the place of the first – the initial layer of perceptible reality' (Lefebvre, 1971), there are, as he goes on to affirm, always 'objections and contradictions which hinder the closing of the circuit' between sign and object, production and reproduction.

We can now return to the meaning of youth subcultures, for the emergence of such groups has signalled in a spectacular fashion the breakdown of consensus in the post-war period. In the following chapters we shall see that it is precisely objections and contradictions of the kind which Lefebvre has described that find expression in subculture. However, the challenge to hegemony which subcultures represent is not issued directly by them. Rather it is expressed obliquely, in style. The objections are lodged, the contradictions displayed (and, as we shall see, 'magically resolved') at the profoundly superficial level of appearances: that is, at the level of signs. For the sign-community, the community of myth-consumers, is not a uniform body. As Volosinov has written, it is cut through by class:

> Class does not coincide with the sign community, i.e. with the totality of users of the same set of signs of ideological communication. Thus various different classes will use one and the same language. As a result, differently oriented accents intersect in every ideological sign. Sign becomes the arena of the class struggle. (Volosinov, 1973)

The struggle between different discourses, different definitions and meanings within ideology is therefore always, at the same time, a struggle within signification: a struggle for possession of the sign which extends to even the most mundane areas of everyday life. To turn once more to the examples used in the Introduction, to the safety pins and tubes of vaseline, we can see that such commodities are indeed open to a double inflection: to 'illegitimate' as well as 'legitimate' uses. These 'humble objects' can be magically appropriated; 'stolen' by subordinate groups and made to carry 'secret' meanings: meanings which express, in code, a form of resistance to the order which guarantees their continued subordination.

Style in subculture is, then, pregnant with significance. Its transformations go 'against nature', interrupting the process of 'normalization'. As such, they are gestures, movements towards a speech which offends the 'silent majority', which challenges the principle of unity and cohesion, which contradicts the myth of consensus. Our task becomes, like Barthes', to discern the hidden messages inscribed in code on the glossy surfaces of style, to trace them out as 'maps of meaning' which obscurely re-present the very contradictions they are designed to resolve or conceal.

Academics who adopt a semiotic approach are not alone in reading significance into the loaded surfaces of life. The existence of spectacular subcultures continually opens up those surfaces to other potentially subversive readings. Jean Genet, the archetype of the 'unnatural' deviant, again exemplifies the practice of resistance through style. He is as convinced in his own way as is Roland Barthes of the ideological character of cultural signs. He is equally oppressed by the seamless web of forms and meanings which encloses and yet excludes him. His reading is equally partial. He makes his own list and draws his own conclusions:

> I was astounded by so rigorous an edifice whose details were united against me. Nothing in the world is irrelevant: the stars on a general's sleeve, the stock-market quotations, the olive harvest, the style of the judiciary, the wheat exchange, the flower-beds, . . . Nothing. This order . . . had a meaning – my exile. (Genet, 1967)

It is this alienation from the deceptive 'innocence' of appearances which gives the teds, the mods, the punks and no doubt future groups of as yet unimaginable 'deviants' the impetus to move from man's second 'false nature' (Barthes, 1972) to a genuinely expressive artifice; a truly subterranean style. As a symbolic violation of the social order, such a movement attracts and will continue to attract attention, to provoke censure and to act, as we shall see, as the fundamental bearer of significance in subculture.

No subculture has sought with more grim determination than the punks to detach itself from the taken-for-granted landscape of normalized forms, nor to bring down upon itself such vehement disapproval. We shall begin therefore with the moment of punk and we shall return to that moment throughout the course of this book. It is perhaps appropriate that the punks, who have made such large claims for illiteracy, who have pushed profanity to such startling extremes, should be used to test some of the methods for 'reading' signs evolved in the centuries-old debate on the sanctity of culture.

PART ONE:
SOME CASE STUDIES

finally broken?) the sun provided seasonal relief from the dreary cycle of doom-laden headlines which had dominated the front pages of the tabloids throughout the winter. Nature performed its statutory ideological function and 'stood in' for all the other 'bad news', provided tangible proof of 'improvement' and pushed aside the strikes and the dissension. With predictable regularity, 'bright young things' were shown flouncing along Oxford Street in harem bags and beach shorts, bikini tops and polaroids in that last uplifting item for the *News at Ten*. The sun served as a 'cheeky' postscript to the crisis: a lighthearted addendum filled with tropical promise. The crisis, too, could have its holiday. But as the weeks and months passed and the heatwave continued, the old mythology of doom and disaster was reasserted with a vengeance. The 'miracle' rapidly became a commonplace, an everyday affair, until one morning in mid-July it was suddenly re-christened a 'freak disorder': a dreadful, last, unlooked-for factor in Britain's decline.

The heatwave was officially declared a drought in August, water was rationed, crops were failing, and Hyde Park's grass burned into a delicate shade of raw sienna. The end was at hand and Last Days imagery began to figure once more in the press. Economic categories, cultural and natural phenomena were confounded with more than customary abandon until the drought took on an almost metaphysical significance. A Minister for Drought was appointed, Nature had now been officially declared 'unnatural', and all the age-old inferences were drawn with an obligatory modicum of irony to keep within the bounds of common sense. In late August, two events of completely different mythical stature coincided to confirm the worst forebodings: it was demonstrated that the excessive heat was threatening the very structure of the nation's houses (cracking the foundations) and the Notting Hill Carnival, traditionally a paradigm of racial harmony, exploded into violence. The Caribbean festival, with all its Cook's Tours connotations of happy, dancing coloured folk, of jaunty bright calypsos and exotic costumes, was suddenly, unaccountably, transformed into a menacing congregation of angry black youths and embattled police. Hordes of young black Britons did the Soweto dash across the nation's television screens and conjured up fearful images of other Negroes, other confrontations, other 'long, hot summers'. The humble dustbin lid, the staple of every steel band, the symbol of the 'carnival spirit', of Negro ingenuity and the resilience of ghetto culture, took on an altogether more ominous significance when used by white-faced policemen as a desperate shield against an angry rain of bricks.

It was during this strange apocalyptic summer that punk made its sensational debut in the music press.[1] In London, especially in the south west and more specifically in the vicinity of the King's Road, a new style was being generated combining elements drawn from a whole range of heterogeneous youth styles. In fact punk claimed a dubious parentage. Strands from David Bowie and glitter-rock were woven together with elements from American proto-punk (the Ramones, the Heartbreakers, Iggy Pop, Richard Hell), from that faction within London pub-rock (the 101-ers, the Gorillas, etc.) inspired by the mod subculture of the 60s, from the Canvey Island 40s revival and the Southend r & b bands (Dr Feelgood, Lew Lewis, etc.), from northern soul and from reggae.

Not surprisingly, the resulting mix was somewhat unstable: all these elements constantly threatened to separate and return to their original sources. Glam rock contributed narcissism, nihilism and gender confusion. American punk offered a minimalist aesthetic (e.g. the Ramones' 'Pinhead' or Crime's 'I Stupid'), the cult of the Street and a penchant for self-laceration. Northern Soul (a genuinely secret subculture of working-class youngsters dedicated to acrobatic dancing and fast American soul of the 60s, which centres on clubs like the Wigan Casino) brought its subterranean tradition of fast, jerky rhythms, solo dance styles and amphetamines; reggae its exotic and dangerous aura of forbidden identity, its conscience, its dread and its cool. Native rhythm 'n blues reinforced the brashness and the speed of Northern Soul, took rock back to the basics and contributed a highly developed iconoclasm, a thoroughly British persona and an extremely selective appropriation of the rock 'n roll heritage.

This unlikely alliance of diverse and superficially incompatible musical traditions, mysteriously accomplished under punk, found ratification in an equally eclectic clothing style which reproduced the same kind of cacophony on the visual level. The whole ensemble, literally safety-pinned together, became the celebrated and highly photogenic phenomenon known as punk which throughout 1977 provided the tabloids with a fund of predictably sensational copy and the quality press with a welcome catalogue of beautifully broken codes. Punk reproduced the entire sartorial history of post-war working-class youth cultures in 'cut up' form, combining elements which had originally belonged to completely different epochs. There was a chaos of quiffs and leather jackets, brothel creepers and winkle pickers, plimsolls and paka macs, moddy crops and skinhead strides, drainpipes and vivid socks, bum freezers and bovver boots – all kept 'in place' and 'out of time' by the spectacular adhesives: the safety pins and plastic clothes pegs, the bondage straps and bits of string which attracted so much horrified and fascinated attention. Punk is therefore a singularly appropriate point of departure for a study of this kind because punk style contained distorted reflections of all the major post-war subcultures. But before we can interpret the significance of these subcultures, we must first unscramble the sequence in which they occurred.

Boredom in Babylon

> Ordinary life is so dull that I get out of it as much as possible. (Steve Jones, a Sex Pistol, quoted in *Melody Maker*)

It seems entirely appropriate that punk's 'unnatural' synthesis should have hit the London streets during that bizarre summer. Apocalypse was in the air and the rhetoric of punk was drenched in apocalypse: in the stock imagery of crisis and sudden change. Indeed, even punk's epiphanies were hybrid affairs, representing the awkward and unsteady confluence of the two radically dissimilar languages of *reggae* and *rock*. As the shock-haired punks began to gather in a shop called Sex on a corner of the King's Road, aptly named the Worlds End, David Bowie's day of the *Diamond Dogs* (R.C.A. Victor, 1974) and the triumph of the 'super-alienated humanoid' was somehow made to coincide with reggae's Day of Judgement, with the overthrow of Babylon and the end of alienation altogether.

It is here that we encounter the first of punk's endemic contradictions, for the visions of apocalypse superficially fused in punk came from essentially antagonistic sources. David Bowie and the New York punk bands had pieced together from a variety of acknowledged 'artistic' sources – from the literary *avant-garde* and the underground cinema – a self-consciously profane and terminal aesthetic. Patti Smith, an American punk and ex-art student, claimed to have invented a new form, 'rock poetry', and incorporated readings from Rimbaud and William Burroughs into her act. Bowie, too, cited Burroughs as an influence and used his famous cut-up technique of random juxtapositions to 'compose' lyrics. Richard Hell drew on the writings of Lautréamont and Huysmans. British punk bands, generally younger and more self-consciously proletarian, remained largely innocent of literature. However, for better or worse, the literary sources turned out to be firmly although implicitly inscribed in the aesthetics of British punk too. Similarly, there were connections (via Warhol and Wayne County in America, via the art school bands like the Who and the Clash in Britain) with underground cinema and *avant-garde* art.

By the early 70s, these tendencies had begun to cohere into a fully fledged nihilist aesthetic and the emergence of this aesthetic together with its characteristic focal concerns (polymorphous, often wilfully perverse sexuality, obsessive individualism, fragmented sense of self, etc.) generated a good deal of controversy amongst those interested in rock culture (see Melly, 1972; Taylor and Wall, 1976). From Jagger in *Performance* (Warner Bros, 1969) to Bowie as the 'thin white duke', the spectre of the dandy 'drowning in his own opera' (Sartre, 1968) has haunted rock from the wings as it were, and in the words of Ian Taylor and Dave Wall 'plays back the alienation of youth onto itself' (1976). Punk represents the most recent phase in this process. In punk, alienation assumed an almost tangible quality. It could almost be grasped. It gave itself up to the cameras in 'blankness', the removal of expression (see any photograph of any punk group), the refusal to speak and be positioned. This trajectory – the solipsism, the neurosis, the cosmetic rage – had its origins in rock.

But at almost every turn the dictates of this profane aesthetic were countermanded by the righteous imperatives of another musical form: reggae. Reggae occupies the other end of that wide spectrum of influences which bore upon punk. As early as May 1977 Jordan, the famous punk shop assistant of Sex and Seditionaries was expressing a preference for reggae over 'new wave' on the pages of the *New Musical Express* (7 May 1977). 'It's the only music we [i.e. Jordan and J. Rotten] dance to'. Although Rotten himself insisted on the relative autonomy of punk and reggae, he displayed a detailed knowledge of the more esoteric reggae numbers in a series of interviews throughout 1977. Most conspicuously amongst punk groups, the Clash were heavily influenced not only by the music, but also by the visual iconography of black Jamaican street style. Khaki battle dress stencilled with the Caribbean legends DUB and HEAVY MANNERS, narrow 'sta-prest' trousers, black brogues and slip ons, even the pork pie hat, were all adopted at different times by various members of the group. In addition, the group played 'White Riot', a song inspired directly by the '76 Carnival, against a screen-printed backdrop of the Notting Hill disturbances, and they toured with a reggae discotheque presided over by Don Letts, the black Rastafarian d-j who shot the documentary film *Punk* while working at the Roxy Club in Covent Garden.

As we shall see, although apparently separate and autonomous, punk and the black British subcultures with which reggae is associated were connected at a deep structural level. But the dialogue between the two forms cannot properly be decoded until the internal composition and significance of both reggae and the British working-class youth cultures which preceded punk are fully understood. This involves two major tasks. First reggae must be traced back to its roots in the West Indies, and second the history of post-war British youth culture must be reinterpreted as a succession of differential responses to the black immigrant presence in Britain from the 1950s onwards. Such a reassessment demands a shift of emphasis away from the normal areas of interest – the school, police, media and parent culture (which have anyway been fairly exhaustively treated by other writers, see, e.g. Hall *et al.*, 1976) – to what I feel to be the largely neglected dimension of race and race relations.

THREE

Are you there Africa with the bulging chest and oblong
thigh? Sulking Africa, wrought of iron in the fire, Africa
of the millions of royal slaves, deported Africa, drifting
continent are you there? Slowly you vanish, you with-
draw into the past, into the tales of castaways, colonial
museums, the works of scholars; but I call you back this
evening to attend a secret revel. (Jean Genet, 1966b)

Back to Africa

THE differences between rock and reggae should be
sufficiently obvious to render exhaustive documenta-
tion unnecessary. It is simply explained here by Mark
Kidel: 'Whereas jazz and rock often reflect an amphetamine frenzy, reggae tunes in to the slowness of ganja'
(review of a Bob Marley concert, *New Statesman*, 8 July
1977). Reggae draws on a quite specific experience (the
experience of black people in Jamaica and Great Britain –
a whole generation of young Black Britons have formed
reggae bands in the last few years, e.g. the Cimarons, Steel
Pulse, Matumbi, Black Slate, Aswaad). It is cast in a unique

style, in a language of its own – Jamaican patois, that
shadow-form, 'stolen' from the Master[1] and mysteriously
inflected, 'decomposed' and reassembled in the passage
from Africa to the West Indies. It moves to more ponderous
and moody rhythms. It 'rocks steady'[2] around a bass-line
which is both more prominent and more austere. Its rhetoric is more densely constructed, and less diverse in origin;
emanating in large part from two related sour s – a distinctively Jamaican oral culture and an equally distinctive
appropriation of the Bible. There are strong elements of
Jamaican pentecostal, of 'possession by the Word', and the
call and response pattern which binds the preacher to his
congregation, is reproduced in reggae.[3] Reggae addresses a
community in transit through a series of retrospective
frames (the Rastafarian movement (see pp. 33–9), the Back
to Africa theme) which reverse the historical sequence of
migrations (Africa–Jamaica–Great Britain). It is the
living record of a people's journey – of the passage from
slavery to servitude – and that journey can be mapped
along the lines of reggae's unique structure.

Africa finds an echo inside reggae in its distinctive per-
cussion. The voice of Africa in the West Indies has traditionally been identified with insurrection and silenced wherever
possible (see Hall, 1975). In particular, the preservation of
African traditions, like drumming, has in the past been construed by the authorities (the Church, the colonial and even
some 'post-colonial' governments) as being intrinsically
subversive, posing a symbolic threat to law and order. These
outlawed traditions were not only considered anti-social and
unchristian, they were positively, triumphantly pagan.
They suggested unspeakable alien rites, they made possible
illicit and rancorous allegiances which smacked of future
discord. They hinted at that darkest of rebellions: a celebration of Negritude. They restored 'deported Africa', that
'drifting continent' to a privileged place within the black
mythology. And the very existence of that mythology was

enough to inspire an immense dread in the hearts of some white slave owners.

Africa thus came to represent for blacks in the Caribbean forbidden territory, a Lost World, a History abandoned to the contradictory Western myths of childhood innocence and man's inherent evil. It became a massive Out of Bounds on the other side of slavery. But beyond this continent of negatives there lay a place where all the utopian and anti-European values available to the dispossessed black could begin to congregate. And paradoxically it was from the Bible – the civilizing agent *par excellence* – that alternative values and dreams of a better life were drawn. It was in Rastafarianism that these two symbolic clusters (Black Africa and the White man's Bible) so ostensibly antithetical, were most effectively integrated. To understand how such a heretical convergence was possible, and how the meta-message in the Christian faith (submission to the Master) was so dramatically transcended, one must first understand how that faith was mediated to the Jamaican black.

The Bible is a central determining force in both reggae music and popular West Indian consciousness in general. In the past, the scriptures had been used by the colonial authorities to inculcate Western values and to introduce the African to European notions of culture, repression, the soul, etc. It was under their sacred auspices that civilization itself was to be achieved: that Western culture was to fulfil its divinely ordained mission of conquest. Underpinned by the persistent dualism of Biblical rhetoric ('Black Satan' and 'the snow-white Lamb of God') slavery could flourish with a relatively clear conscience, transforming the 'savage' into an industrious servant, interpolating order and the godly virtues between the dispossessed African and his mutinous 'nature'.

However, this internal colonization was by necessity partial and flawed. As the years went by it became increasingly obvious that there was a distinction between the practice of slavery and the Christian ideology which had originally 'explained' it. The contradictions became increasingly difficult to contain. Inevitably, the black community began to seek its own reflection in the Biblical texts, and the openness of the religious metaphors invited just such a set of identifications. The Bible had its dark side too: an 'Africa' which lay dormant and forgotten inside the language of the white Master. Read between the lines the Text could be made to deliver up this Africa, to free it, and restore it to the 'righteous sufferer'.

Of course, the Biblical story is readily amenable to exclusively black interpretations.[4] It supplies in particular a whole range of peculiarly appropriate metaphors for the condition of poor, black, working-class West Indians (Babylon, the suffering Israelites) and a complementary set of metaphorical answers to the problems which define that condition (delivery of the Righteous, retribution for the Wicked, Judgement Day, Zion, the Promised Land). It catalogues precisely and at length the trials and tribulations of slavery (the history of the Jewish nation) and recommends an immediate internal 'healing of the breach' between pain and desire (through faith, grace, the Holy Spirit, etc.). Not only specific archetypes but the characteristic modes of discourse in which those archetypes are generally situated (the parable, the aphorism, etc.) have influenced West Indian consciousness at the profoundest levels providing the most supple and expressive frames of reference.

The Rastafarian solution

In this way, the Bible has meshed together with the oral culture of Jamaica, performing a primary semantic function, serving as a model for all literature (the Word of God). It can be made to 'mean all things equivocally' (Alfred Jarry, quoted in Shattuck, 1969). It is the supremely ambiguous means through which the black community can most readily make sense of its subordinate position within an alien society.

The Rastafarians believe that the accession of Haille Selassie to the throne of Ethiopia in 1930 represented the fulfilment of Biblical and secular prophecies concerning the imminent downfall of 'Babylon' (i.e. the white colonial powers) and the deliverance of the black races.

It is apt that such a tradition of passionate heterodoxy, having generated so many 'contained' readings of the impoverished Jamaican's material condition should eventually produce the Rastafarian solution: the appropriation which removes the dark kernel from its European shell, which finds an 'Africa' marooned on the pages of the Bible. For Rastafarianism is a reading which threatens to explode the sacred Text itself, to challenge the very Word of the Father.

The profound subversion of the white man's Religion which places God in Ethiopia and the black 'sufferer' in Babylon has proved singularly appealing to working-class youth in both the ghettos of Kingston and the West Indian communities of Great Britain. This appeal requires little explanation. Clothed in dreadlocks[5] and 'righteous ire' the Rastaman effects a spectacular resolution of the material contradictions which oppress and define the West Indian community. He deciphers 'sufferation', that key term in the expressive vocabulary of ghetto culture, naming its historical causes (colonialism, economic exploitation) and promising deliverance through exodus to 'Africa'. He is the living refutation of Babylon (contemporary capitalist society), refusing to deny his stolen history. By a perverse and wilful transformation, he turns poverty and exile into 'signs of grandeur',* tokens of his own esteem, tickets which will take him home to Africa and Zion when Babylon is over-

* 'The most sordid signs became for me the signs of grandeur', Genet, 1967.

thrown. Most importantly, he traces out his 'roots' in red, green and gold,* dissolving the gulf of centuries which separates the West Indian community from its past, and from a positive evaluation of its blackness.

Until the late 60s at least, the Rastas were persecuted for accentuating the very differences of race and class which the newly independent Jamaican government sought so desperately to conceal.[6] However, under the more sympathetic Manley regime[7] the Rastafarians have been granted a kind of recognition which signals the beginnings of what has been described as a 'cultural revolution' (interview with Stuart Hall, Radio 3, July 1977), a generalized shift in patterns of industrial as well as ideological development[8] away from Europe and America towards Cuba and the Third World. This shift coincides exactly with the evolution of the Jamaican popular music industry; and reggae has proved an ideal medium for the Rasta 'message'.

Reggae and Rastafarianism

Even in the *ska* records of the early 60s, underneath the 'rudeness' and the light, choppy metre, there was a thread of Rastafarianism (Don Drummond, Reco, etc.) which became increasingly noticeable as the decade wore on until the Rasta contingent within reggae began, more or less exclusively, to determine the direction the music was to take. Reggae began to slow down to an almost African metabolism. The lyrics became more self-consciously Jamaican, more dimly enunciated and overgrown until they disappeared altogether in the 'dub',[9] to be replaced by 'talk-over'. The 'dread', the ganja, the Messianic feel of this 'heavy' reggae, its blood and fire rhetoric, its troubled

* The colours of the Ethiopian flag emblazoned on items as various as badges, cardigans, shirts, sandals, tams (woollen hats), walking sticks ('rods of correction').

rhythms can all be attributed to the Rasta influence. And it was largely through reggae, played at local 'sound-systems' (i.e. discotheques frequented by black working-class youth) and available only through an underground network of small retailers, that the Rastafarian ethos, the 'dreadlocks' and 'ethnicity' were communicated to members of the West Indian community in Great Britain.

For the unemployed black youth, 'heavy dub' and 'rockers'[10] provided an alternative sound-track, infinitely preferable to the muzak which filled the vast new shopping precincts where he spent his days 'doing nothing',* subjected to the random tyrannies of 'sus'.† But of course the original religious meanings of Rastafarianism suffered adjustment in the transition.

Somewhere between Trenchtown and Ladbroke Grove, the cult of Rastafari had become a 'style': an expressive combination of 'locks', of khaki camouflage and 'weed' which proclaimed unequivocally the alienation felt by many young black Britons. Alienation could scarcely be avoided: it was built into the lives of young working-class West Indians in the form of bad housing, unemployment and police harassment. As early as 1969, it had been estimated that white youngsters from equivalent backgrounds were approximately five times more likely to find skilled work (*Observer*, 14 July 1968). In addition, throughout the 60s, relations with the police had been deteriorating steadily. The Mangrove trial of 1969 marked the beginning of a long series of bitter confrontations between the black community and the authorities (the Carib trial, the Oval trial, the 1976 Carnival) which led to a progressive polarization.

It was during this period of growing disaffection and joblessness, at a time when conflict between black youths

* See Corrigan, 1976, who maintains that the major problem experienced by 'kids' is how to 'kill time'.

† Arrested under the 'Suspected Persons' Act; see *Time Out*, 5 August 1977.

and the police was being openly acknowledged in the press, that imported reggae music began to deal directly with problems of race and class, and to resurrect the African heritage. Reggae, and the forms which had preceded it, had always alluded to these problems obliquely. Oppositional values had been mediated through a range of rebel archetypes: the 'rude boy',[11] the gunfighter, the trickster, etc. – which remained firmly tied to the *particular* and tended to celebrate the *individual* status of revolt.

With dub and heavy reggae, this rebellion was given a much wider currency: it was generalized and theorized. Thus, the rude boy hero immortalized in ska and rocksteady – the lone delinquent pitched hopelessly against an implacable authority – was supplanted as the central focus of identity by the Rastafarian who broke the Law in more profound and subtle ways. Not only did the Rasta fix the dreary cycle of solitary refusal and official retribution within the context of Jamaica's absent history, he broke that cycle altogether by installing the conflict elsewhere on the neglected surfaces of everyday life. By questioning the neat articulations of common sense (in appearance, in language, etc.) the Rasta was able to carry the crusade beyond the obvious arena of law and order to the level of the 'obvious' itself. It was here, quite literally on the 'skin' of the social formation, that the Rastafarian movement made its most startling innovations, refracting the system of black and white polarities, turning negritude into a positive sign, a loaded essence, a weapon at once deadly and divinely licensed. The process of adjustment which simultaneously intensified conflict and turned it inwards was reflected in the music and reproduced exactly in musical form. As has been said, reggae became darker and more African, the patois even more impenetrable, the menace more overt. At the same time, the 'Battle(s) on Orange Street' (ska record by Prince Buster), literal, bloody and yet humourously described in the 60s, were replaced by full-scale 'War inna

Babylon' (Max Romeo, Island, 1976). This 'war' had a double nature: it was fought around ambiguous terms of reference which designated both an actual and an imaginary set of relations (race–class nexus/Babylon; economic exploitation/Biblical suffering), a struggle both real and metaphorical, which described a world of forms enmeshed in ideology where appearance and illusion were synonomous.

Of course, war had its dubious compensations too: a sense of solidarity and purpose, an identity, an enemy more or less clearly defined. Even the tension between violent and religious 'solutions' could be reduced if the conflict between the 'Police and (the) Thieves' 'scaring the Nation with their guns and ammunition' (Junior Murvin, Island, 1977) was taken not only to complement but to *signify* the bloodless battle being waged by the Rastafarians on the terrain of ideology. This displacement was more easily accomplished the further one moved from the original sources of reggae and Rastafarianism. In Great Britain, at every local 'sound-system', in every major city where immigrants had settled in sufficient numbers, a righteous army of militant sufferers would gather to pledge allegiance to the Ethiopian flag.

The 'sound-system', perhaps more than any other institution within working-class West Indian life, was the site at which blackness could be most thoroughly explored, most clearly and uncompromisingly expressed. To a community hemmed in on all sides by discrimination, hostility, suspicion and blank incomprehension, the sound-system came to represent, particularly for the young, a precious inner sanctum, uncontaminated by alien influences, a black heart beating back to Africa on a steady pulse of dub. In clubs like the Four Aces, in the Seven Sisters Road, North London, an exclusively black audience would 'stare down' Babylon, carried along on a thunderous bass-line, transported on 1000 watts. Power was at home here – just beyond the finger tips. It hung on the air – invisible, electric – channelled through a battery of home-made speakers. It was present in every 'toasted'[12] incantation. In an atmosphere shaking with sound, charged with smoke and nemesis, it was easy to imagine that the 'Day of Reckoning' was at hand; that when, at last, the 'lightning flashed', the 'weak heart' would 'drop and the righteous black man stand' ('Lightning Flash', Big Youth, Klik, 1975) armoured in dread,[13] oblivious to his former suffering.

The sound-system thus became associated with the heavier more 'rootsy' forms of reggae. The two became mutually dependent; indeed they were, for all practical purposes, identical. The music itself was virtually exiled from the airwaves. It could live only in and through the cumbersome network of cabinets and wires, valves and microphones which make up the 'system' and which, though legally the property of an individual entrepreneur, was owned in a much deeper sense by the community. And it was through music, more than any other medium, that the communication with the past, with Jamaica, and hence Africa, considered vital for the maintenance of black identity, was possible. The 'system' turned on sound; the sound was intimately bound up with the notion of 'culture'; and if the system was attacked then the community itself was symbolically threatened. It thus became hallowed ground, territory to be defended against possible contamination by white groups. Police interference was, of course, vehemently resented and in some cases the mere presence of policemen was sufficient to provoke black youths to violent reprisal. The Notting Hill riot of 1976[14] and the Carib Club incident of 1974[15] can be interpreted in this way, as symbolic defences of communal space.

Exodus: A double crossing

Fortunately relations with the larger white community were in general rather less fraught. In some parts of London, at least, there existed a whole network of subterranean channels which had for years linked the fringes of the indigenous population to the equivalent West Indian subcultures. Originally opened up to the illicit traffic of 'weed' and jazz, these internal channels provided the basis for much broader cultural exchanges. The bonds were strengthened by time and a common experience of privation, by lives spent in close proximity around a similar set of focal concerns. While each preserved its own distinctive shape, the two cultures could harmonize around the mutual interlocking loyalties of family and street, pub and neighbourhood. With significant exceptions (Nottingham and Notting Hill in 1958, Hoxton and parts of the East End in the 70s) a pattern of relatively peaceful coexistence began to emerge. Certainly this was true of the 50s and early 60s. In general, the first generation West Indian immigrants held too much cultural space in common with their white working-class neighbours to allow any open antagonism to develop. Confirmed Anglophiles, even when 'at home' in Jamaica, they shared the same goals, sought the same diversions (a pint of beer, a game of darts, a dance on Saturday night) and, despite the unfamiliar accent, drew upon the same 'language of fatalism',[16] resigned to their lowly position, confident that their children would enjoy better prospects, better lives. Of course, things failed to improve at the expected rate and by the early 70s full employment appeared a remote possibility indeed; a moment dimly remembered and by no means representative of Britain's economic fortunes since the War.

Meanwhile black children born and educated in this country were rather less inclined than their parents either to accept the inferior status and narrow options offered them, or to leave unquestioned the dominant definitions of their blackness. Reggae provided the focus around which another culture, another set of values and self-definitions could cluster. These changes were subtly registered in the style of black youth; in the gait, the manner, the voice which seemed almost overnight to become less anglicized.

The very way the black youth moved implied a new assurance – there was more deliberate 'sass', more spring, less shuffle.[17] The clothes had also undergone a series of significant adjustments over the years. The aspirations of the early immigrants had been mirrored in the rainbow mohair suits and picture ties, the neatly printed frocks and patent-leather shoes which they had worn on their arrival in Great Britain. Each snowy cuff had reflected a desire to succeed, to 'make the grade' in the terms traditionally laid down by white society, just as, with tragic irony, all hopes of ever really fitting in were inadvertently belied by every garish jacket sleeve – too loud and jazzy for contemporary British tastes. Both the dreams and the disappointments of an entire generation were thus inscribed in the very cut (ambitious and improbable) of the clothes in which it chose to make its entrance.

The crossing to Great Britain was, like most voluntary migrations, an act of faith: an exodus. It required a peculiar blend of contradictory motivations: desperation or at least impatience with the host country, a belief in the efficacy of action, a desire for increased status, and confidence that the Mother Country would recognize its obligations, would welcome and reward its lost children.

For the first wave of immigrants, which comprised mainly skilled and semi-skilled men, the drive towards improvement was tempered with conservatism: a belief that Britain was bound, by the decency and justice with which it was conventionally associated in Jamaica, to supply a reasonable standard of living for those prepared to work. Typically, the West Indian immigrants of the 50s wanted jobs, homes, respectability, a place for the family to settle once and for all. On the other hand, those that followed in the 60s tended to be unskilled and were, perhaps, more straightforwardly desperate: dissatisfied with the little Jamaica had to offer (Hiro, 1972). For these, the movement to England represented both a last-ditch attempt to salvage something worthwhile from life and a 'magical' solution to their problems. Perhaps because there was less to lose, more was invested in the transition from the West Indies to Great Britain: hopes of an almost religious nature and intensity were pinned on the outcome. The disillusion felt by this second wave of immigrants therefore tended to be correspondingly deeper, more final and more readily expressed. In any case, as the immigrants began to congregate in the decaying inner rings of Britain's larger cities, a new West Indian style began to emerge. This style was less painfully hemmed in by British-ness, less torn between sobriety and 'colour', and behind it there lay the suggestion (unwelcome to white eyes) that yet another migration had taken place, that Britain had failed to supply the promised goods, and that the disaffected immigrants had psychologically moved out.

On the deviant margins of West Indian society, at least, there were significant changes in appearance. The hustlers and street-corner men, encouraged perhaps by the growth of black clubs and discotheques in the mid-60s, were sharpening up, combining hats and 'shades' and Italian suits to produce a West Indian equivalent of the U.S. 'soul-brother' look; tight-fitting, loose-limbed, black and yet urbane. This soul brother moved on the cool lines of jazz, ska and American r & b. He reproduced the timbre and the scansion of these forms in his walk and argot. He sought refuge in their dark interiors from the world of 'straights' and whites. In these ways, he reassessed the stigmata and turned Caribbean flashiness into a declaration of alien intent, a sign of his Otherness. It was largely under his auspices that blackness was recuperated and made symbolically available to young West Indian men. This blackness was unwrapped from and through the music of the 60s; it was teased up to the surface in *avant-garde* jazz (e.g. John Coltrane, Miles Davis, Pharoah Saunders, Archie Shepp), and (more importantly here) in dub and heavy reggae.

Of course, this development had its visual corollary in

dress. During the 70s, the 'youth' were developing their own unique style: a refracted form of Rastafarian aesthetic, borrowed from the sleeves of imported reggae albums and inflected to suit the needs of second-generation immigrants. This was a Rastafarianism at more than one remove, stripped of nearly all its original religious meanings: a distillation, a highly selective appropriation of all those elements within Rastafarianism which stressed the importance of resistance and black identity, and which served to position the black man and his 'queen' outside the dominant white ideology. The difference around which the whole Rasta style revolved was literally inscribed on the skin of black people and it was through appearance that this difference was to be extended, elaborated upon, realized. Those young blacks who 'stepped' to 'Humble Lion'[19] began to cultivate a more obviously African 'natural' image.[20] The pork-pie hat disappeared to be replaced by the roughly woven 'tam'. Tonic, mohair and terylene – the raw material for all those shiny suits in midnight and electric blue – were exchanged for cotton, wool and denim out of which more casual and serviceable garments were made. On every other British high street stood an army-surplus store which supplied the righteous with battle dress and combat jackets: a whole wardrobe of sinister guerilla chic. The rude boy crop was grown out and allowed to explode into an ethnic 'Afro' frizz, or plaited into 'locks' or 'knots' (the ubiquitous natty or knotty style). Girls began to leave their hair unstraightened, short or plaited into intricately parted arabesques, capillary tributes to an imagined Africa.

All these developments were mediated to those members of the white working class who lived in the same areas, worked in the same factories and schools and drank in adjacent pubs. In particular, the trajectory 'back to Africa' within second-generation immigrant youth culture was closely monitored by those neighbouring white youths interested in forming their own subcultural options. Of course,

in both Britain and America relations between black and
white youth cultures have always been delicate, charged
with a potentially explosive significance, irrespective of
whether or not any actual contact takes place between the
two groups. There are strong symbolic links which can be
translated into empathy ('For us the whole coloured race
was sacred' – George Melly, 1970) or emulation (e.g. hard
drug use in the modern jazz era[21]). Both Paul Goodman
(1968) and Jock Young (1971) have characterized the Negro
as the quintessential subterranean, embodying all those
values (the search for adventure and excitement) which
coexist with and undercut the sober positives of mainstream
society (routinization, security, etc.). In these terms, the
positions 'youth' and 'Negro' are often aligned in the
dominant mythology. As Jock Young (1971) writes: They
are 'viewed with the same ambivalence: happy-go-lucky
and lazy, hedonistic and dangerous'.

Of course, at different times and in different circumstances, this congruence can be more or less apparent, more
or less actively perceived and experienced. Put in general
terms, identification between the two groups can be either
open or closed, direct or indirect, acknowledged or un-
acknowledged. It can be recognized and extended into
actual links (the mods, skinheads and punks) or repressed
and inverted into an antagonism (teds, greasers). In either
case, the relationship represents a crucial determining
factor in the evolution of each youth cultural form and in
the ideology both signified in that form and 'acted out' by its
members.

At another level, patterns of rejection and assimilation
between host and immigrant communities can be mapped
along the spectacular lines laid down by white working-class
youth cultures. The succession of white subcultural forms
can be read as a series of deep-structural adaptations which
symbolically accommodate or expunge the black presence
from the host community. It is on the plane of aesthetics: in

dress, dance, music; in the whole rhetoric of style, that we find the dialogue between black and white most subtly and comprehensively recorded, albeit in code. By describing, interpreting and deciphering these forms, we can construct an oblique account of the exchanges which have taken place between the two communities. We can watch, played out on the loaded surfaces of British working-class youth cultures, a phantom history of race relations since the War.

FOUR

At lilac evening I walked with every muscle aching amongst the lights of 27th and Welton in the Denver coloured section wishing I were a Negro, feeling that the best the white world has offered me was not enough ecstasy for me, not enough life, joy, kicks, darkness, music, not enough night. (Jack Kerouac, 1958)

Hipsters, beats and teddy boys

THE bonds which link white youth cultures to the black urban working class have long been recognized by commentators on the American popular music scene. There is a well-documented tradition of miscegenation in jazz. Many white musicians have 'jammed' with black artists while others have borrowed (some would say stolen) the music, translated and transferred it to a different context. The structure and meaning of jazz has been modified in the process. As the music fed into mainstream popular culture during the 20s and 30s, it tended to become bowdlerized, drained of surplus eroticism, and any hint of anger or recrimination blown along the 'hot' lines was delicately refined into inoffensive night club sound. White swing represents the climax of this process: innocuous, generally unobtrusive, possessing a broad appeal, it was a laundered product which contained none of the subversive connotations of its original black sources.[1] These suppressed meanings were, however, triumphantly reaffirmed in be-bop,[2] and by the mid-50s a new, younger white audience began to see itself reflected darkly in the dangerous, uneven surfaces of contemporary *avant-garde*, despite the fact that the musicians responsible for the New York sound[3] deliberately sought to restrict white identification by producing a jazz which was difficult to listen to and even more difficult to imitate. None the less, the 'beat' and the hipster began to improvise their own exclusive styles around a less compromised form of jazz: a jazz of 'pure abstraction' which 'short-circuited the obvious'.[4]

This unprecedented convergence of black and white, so aggressively, so unashamedly proclaimed, attracted the inevitable controversy which centred on the predictable themes of race, sex, rebellion, etc., and which rapidly developed into a moral panic. All the classic symptoms of hysteria most commonly associated with the emergence of rock 'n roll a few years later were present in the outraged reaction with which conservative America greeted the beat and the hipster,[5] and at the same time a whole mythology of the Black Man and his Culture was being developed by sympathetic liberal observers. Here the Negro was blowing free, untouched by the dreary conventions which tyrannized more fortunate members of society (i.e. the writers) and, although trapped in a cruel environment of mean streets and tenements, by a curious inversion he also emerged the ultimate victor. He escaped emasculation and the bounded existential possibilities which middle-class life offered. Immaculate in poverty, he lived out the blocked options of a generation of white radical intellectuals. The Black Man, mistily observed through the self-consciously topical prose of Norman Mailer or the breathless panegyrics of Jack Kerouac (who carried the idealization of Negro culture to almost ludicrous extremes in his novels) could serve for white youth as the model of freedom-in-bondage. Saint and exile, he flew like Charlie 'Bird' above his wretched condition, expressing and transcending contradictions through his art in every solo statement blown (God knows how!) through every battered sax.

Although the hipster and beat subcultures grew out of the same basic mythology, the two styles drew on black culture in different ways and were positioned differently in relation to that culture. According to Goldman:

> . . . the hipster was . . . [a] typical lower-class dandy, dressed up like a pimp, affecting a very cool, cerebral tone – to distinguish him from the gross, impulsive types that surrounded him in the ghetto – and aspiring to the finer things in life, like very good 'tea', the finest of sounds – jazz or Afro-Cuban . . . [whereas] . . . the Beat was originally some earnest middle-class college boy like Kerouac, who was stifled by the cities and the culture he had inherited and who wanted to cut out for distant and exotic places, where he could live like the 'people', write, smoke and meditate. (Goldman, 1974)

The hipster style was assembled in relatively close proximity to the ghetto black: it gave formal expression to an experienced bond, it shared a certain amount of communal space, a common language, and revolved around similar focal concerns. The beat, on the other hand, lived an imaginary relation to the Negro-as-noble-savage, to that heroic Black poised, according to the mythology, between a 'life of constant humility' and 'everthreatening danger', between servitude and freedom (Mailer, 1968). Thus, although the hipster and beat subcultures were organized around a shared identity with blacks (symbolized in jazz), the nature of this identity, exposed in the styles adopted by the two groups, was qualitatively different. The zoot suits and lightweight 'continentals' of the hipster embodied the traditional aspirations (making out and moving up) of the black street-corner man, whereas the beat, studiously ragged in jeans and sandals, expressed a magical relation to a poverty which constituted in his imagination a divine essence, a state of grace, a sanctuary. In both cases, as Iain Chambers has argued, '. . . embedded in black culture, in black music, are oppositional values which in a fresh context served to symbolise and symptomatise the contradictions and tensions played out in [white] youth subculture' (Chambers, 1976).

Of course, as Chambers points out, this transference of values and meanings still holds when we turn to British youth cultures. None the less, it should hardly surprise us that the beat subculture alone, the product of a somewhat romantic alignment with black people, should survive the transition from America to Britain in the 50s. Without a significant black presence in Britain's working-class communities, the equivalent hipster option was simply not available. The influx of West Indian immigrants had only just begun, and when, at last, their influence on British working-class subcultures was felt in the early 60s, it was generally articulated in and through specifically Caribbean forms (ska, bluebeat, etc.). Meanwhile, another more spectacular convergence had occurred outside jazz in rock, and it was not until black gospel and blues had fused with white country and western to produce a completely new form – rock 'n roll – that the line between the two positions (black and British working-class youth) could be surreptitiously elided.

However, in the early days of rock such a symbolic alliance was by no means assured. The music had been taken out of its original context where the implications of the potentially explosive equation of 'Negro' and 'youth' had been fully recognized by the parent culture[6] and transplanted to Britain where it served as the nucleus for the teddy boy style. Here, it existed in a kind of vacuum as a stolen form – a focus for an illicit delinquent identity. It was heard in the vacant lots of the new British coffee bars where, although filtered through a distinctively English atmosphere of boiled milk and beverages, it remained demonstrably alien and futuristic – as baroque as the juke box on which it was played. And like those other sacred artefacts – the quiffs, the drapes, the Brylcreem and the 'flicks' – it came to mean America, a fantasy continent of Westerns and gangsters, luxury, glamour and 'automobiles'.

Effectively excluded and temperamentally detached from the respectable working class, condemned in all probability to a lifetime of unskilled work (Jefferson, 1976a), the teddy boy found himself on the outside in fantasy. He visibly bracketed off the drab routines of school, the job and home by affecting an exaggerated style which juxtaposed two blatantly plundered forms (black rhythm and blues and the aristocratic Edwardian style) (Jefferson, 1976b). In such a context, the 'hollow cosmos' effect of the early rock recordings which Hoggart (1958) mentions was singularly appropriate: in barely audible tones, in a language familiar only through the cinema, they described a distant world the appeal of which must have been considerably enhanced by its very remoteness, its unapproachability (listen, e.g.; to 'Heartbreak Hotel', Elvis Presley, or 'Be Bop a Lula,' Gene Vincent).

In the face of what was necessarily a somewhat crude and cerebral appropriation, the subtle dialogue between black and white musical forms which framed the trembling vocals was bound to go unheard. The history of rock's construction was, after all, easily concealed. It appeared to be merely the latest in a long chain of American novelties (jazz, the hula hoop, the internal combustion engine, popcorn) which embodied in concrete form the 'liberated' drives of New World capitalism. Erupting on the British scene in the late 50s, rock seemed to be spontaneously generated, an immediate expression of youthful energies which was entirely self-explanatory. And when the teddy boys, far from welcoming the newly arrived coloured immigrants, began actively taking up arms against them, they were impervious to any sense of contradiction.

For whatever reasons,[7] teds were frequently involved in unprovoked attacks on West Indians and figured prominently in the 1958 race riots. Neither were relations with the beatniks particularly amicable, and despite the Giles cartoons which regularly depicted beats and teds joining ranks against legions of perpetually flustered bowler-hatted 'gents', there is no evidence of any conspicuous fraternization between the two younger groups. The subcultures were in fact literally worlds apart. The college campuses and dimly lit coffee bars and pubs of Soho and Chelsea were bus rides away from the teddy boy haunts deep in the traditionally working-class areas of south and east London. While the beatnik grew out of a literate, verbal culture, professed an interest in the *avant-garde* (abstract painting, poetry, French existentialism) and affected a bemused cosmopolitan air of bohemian tolerance, the ted was uncompromisingly proletarian and xenophobic. The styles were incompatible, and when 'trad' jazz emerged as the focus for a major British subculture in the late 50s,[8] these differences were even more heavily underlined.

Trad depended on a beery 'blokeish' ambience which was at odds with the angular, nervous, edgy qualities of early rock 'n roll, and the teds' shamelessly fabricated aesthetic – an aggressive combination of sartorial exotica (suede shoes, velvet and moleskin collars, and bootlace ties) – existed in stark contrast to the beatniks' 'natural' blend of dufflecoats, sandals and the C.N.D. Perhaps the teds were further alienated by the beats' implied affiliation to the black cause, an affiliation occasionally extended through the reefer trade and modern jazz into actual contact.

Home-grown cool: The style of the mods

By the early 60s, however, sizeable immigrant communities had been established in Britain's working-class areas, and some kind of rapport between blacks and neighbouring white groups had become possible.

The mods were the first in a long line of working-class youth cultures which grew up around the West Indians, responded positively to their presence and sought to emulate their style. Like the American hipster described above, the mod was a 'typical lower-class dandy' (Goldman, 1974) obsessed with the small details of dress (Wolfe, 1966), defined, like Tom Wolfe's pernickety New York lawyers[9] in the angle of a shirt collar, measured as precisely as the vents in his custom-made jacket; by the shape of his hand-made shoes.

Unlike the defiantly obtrusive teddy boys, the mods were more subtle and subdued in appearance: they wore apparently conservative suits in respectable colours, they were fastidiously neat and tidy. Hair was generally short and clean, and the mods preferred to maintain the stylish contours of an impeccable 'French crew' with invisible lacquer rather than with the obvious grease favoured by the more overtly masculine rockers. The mods invented a style which enabled them to negotiate smoothly between school, work and leisure, and which concealed as much as it stated. Quietly disrupting the orderly sequence which leads from signifier to signified, the mods undermined the conventional meaning of 'collar, suit and tie', pushing neatness to the point of absurdity. They made themselves like Ronald Blythe's discontented labourers[10] into 'masterpieces': they were a little *too* smart, somewhat *too* alert, thanks to amphetamines. And as Dave Laing remarks (1969) 'there was something in the way they moved which adults couldn't make out'; some intangible detail (a polished upper, the brand of a cigarette, the way a tie was knotted) which seemed strangely out of place in the office or class-room.

Somewhere on the way home from school or work, the mods went 'missing': they were absorbed into a 'noonday underground' (Wolfe, 1969) of cellar clubs, discotheques, boutiques and record shops which lay hidden beneath the 'straight world' against which it was ostensibly defined. An integral part of the 'secret identity' constructed here beyond the limited experiential scope of the bosses and teachers, was an emotional affinity with black people (both here and, via soul music, in the U.S.A.): an affinity which was transposed into style. The hard-core Soho mod of 1964, inscrutable behind his shades and 'stingy brim' only deigned to tap his feet (encased in 'basket weaves' or Raoul's originals) to the more esoteric soul imports (Tony Clarke's '(I'm the) Entertainer', James Brown's 'Papa's Got a Brand New Bag', Dobie Gray's '(I'm in with) The In Crowd' or Jamaican ska (Prince Buster's 'Madness')). More firmly embedded than either the teds or the rockers in a variety of jobs[11] which made fairly stringent demands on their appearance, dress and 'general demeanour' as well as their time, the mods placed a correspondingly greater emphasis on the week-end. They lived in between the leaves of the commercial calendar, as it were (hence the Bank Holiday occasions, the week-end events, the 'all-niters'), in the pockets of free time which alone made work meaningful. During these leisure periods (painfully extended, in some cases, through amphetamine) there was real 'work' to be done: scooters to be polished, records to be bought, trousers to be pressed, tapered or fetched from the cleaners, hair to be washed and blow-dried (not just any old hair-drier would do, according to a mod interviewed by the *Sunday Times* in August 1964, it had to be 'one with a hood').

In the midst of all this frantic activity, the Black Man was a constant, serving symbolically as a dark passage down into an imagined 'underworld . . . situated beneath the familiar surfaces of life'[12] where another order was disclosed: a beautifully intricate system in which the values, norms and conventions of the 'straight' world were inverted.

Here, beneath the world's contempt, there were different priorities: work was insignificant, irrelevant; vanity and arrogance were permissible, even desirable qualities, and a more furtive and ambiguous sense of masculinity could be seen to operate. It was the Black Man who made all this possible: by a kind of sorcery, a sleight of hand, through 'soul', he had stepped outside the white man's comprehension. Even as the Entertainer he was still, like the mods, in service to the Man and yet he was a past master in the gentle arts of escape and subversion. He could bend the rules to suit his own purposes, he could elaborate his own private codes and skills and a language which was at once brilliant and opaque: a mask of words: 'a crest and a spurs'.[13] He could inhabit a structure, even alter its shape without ever once owning it, and throughout the mid-6os he provided the hidden inspirational stimulus ('outta sight' in the words of James Brown) for the whole mod style.

By 1964, a mod could say:

At the moment we're hero-worshipping the Spades – they can dance and sing. . . . We do the shake and the hitch-hiker to fast numbers but we're going back to dancing close because the Spades do it. (Hamblett and Deverson, 1964)

White skins, black masks

By 1966, the mod 'movement', subject to the concerted pressures of the media, market forces, and the familiar set of internal contradictions (between keeping private and going public, between staying young and growing up) was beginning to break down into a number of different scenes.

Most noticeably, there was a polarization between the 'hard mods' and those overtly interested in fashion and the 6os 'look'. As Stan Cohen (1972b) observes 'the more extravagant mods . . . involved in the whole rhythm and blues, camp, Carnaby Street scene . . . [were] . . . merging into the fashion-conscious hippies' and the incipient Underground, while the ' "hard mods" (wearing heavy boots, jeans with braces, short hair . . . jumpy . . . on the paranoic edge)' began to turn away from the fancy arabesques of acid rock to champion ska, rocksteady and reggae.

The skinheads grew out of this latter group, and by the late 6os they constituted an identifiable subculture. Aggressively proletarian, puritanical and chauvinist, the skinheads dressed down in sharp contrast to their mod antecedents in a uniform which Phil Cohen (1972a) has described as a 'kind of caricature of the model worker': cropped hair, braces, short, wide levi jeans or functional sta-prest trousers, plain or striped button-down Ben Sherman shirts and highly polished Doctor Marten boots. The skinhead ensemble, as Phil Cohen points out, seems to represent a 'metastatement about the whole process of social mobility' produced by the systematic exaggeration of those elements within the mod style which were self-evidently proletarian, and a complementary suppression of any imagined bourgeois influences (suits, ties, lacquer, 'prettiness'). Phil Cohen goes on to interpret this transformation in terms of 'upward' and 'downward' options: '. . . whereas the mods explored the upwardly mobile option, the skinheads explored the lumpen' (1972a).

In order to express a more stringent 'lumpen' identity, the skinheads drew on two ostensibly incompatible sources: the cultures of the West Indian immigrants and the white working class. A somewhat mythically conceived image of the traditional working-class community with its classic focal concerns, its acute sense of territory, its tough exteriors, its dour 'machismo' (an image which as Cohen says

(1972a) had been 'distorted through middle-class per-
ceptions') was overlaid with elements taken directly from the
West Indian community (and more particularly from the
rude boy subculture of the black delinquent young).
Superimposed one on top of the other, these two very
different traditions coalesced around the skinheads' visual
style which simultaneously embodied both: the clean-cut,
neatly pressed delinquent look owed at least as much to the
rude boys as it did to the 'formalised and very "hard"
stereotypes of the white lumpen males' which have been
stressed in so many accounts of the skinhead phenomenon
(Clarke and Jefferson, 1976).

In such accounts, the black contribution tends to be
played down: confined solely to the influence of reggae
music, whereas the skinheads borrowed individual items
of dress (the crombie, the crop), argot and style directly
from equivalent West Indian groups. Thus, while I agree
with John Clarke and Tony Jefferson (1976) that this 'style
attempted to revive, in symbolic form, some of the ex-
pressions of traditional working-class culture' (see also
Clarke, 1976), the unique and paradoxical manner in
which this revival was accomplished should also be noted.
It was not only by congregating on the all-white football
terraces but through consorting with West Indians at the
local youth clubs and on the street corners, by copying *their*
mannerisms, adopting *their* curses, dancing to *their* music
that the skinheads 'magically recovered' the lost sense of
working-class community. Here we find a dramatic demonstration of the thesis put forward in *Resistance Through
Rituals* (Hall *et al.*, 1976a) that the 'subcultural response'
represents a synthesis on the level of style of those 'forms of
adaptation, negotiation and resistance elaborated by the
parent culture' and others 'more immediate, conjunctural,
specific to youth and its situation and activities'. In the case
of the skinheads, 'things' (dress and value system) taken
from the located parent culture were not only transformed

when placed within the context of a specific generational group; they were, in some cases, radically subverted. The endlessly stretched vowels of Alf Garnett, the absolute epitome of working-class narrowness and racial bigotry were further inflected (and *undercut*) by the smattering of patois (ya raas!) picked up by every self-respecting skinhead from reggae records, and from West Indian colleagues at school and work. Even the skinhead 'uniform' was profoundly ambiguous in origin. The dialectical interplay of black and white 'languages' (dress, argot, focal concerns: style) was clearly expressed in the boots, sta-prest and severely cropped hair: an ensemble which had been composed on the cusp of the two worlds, embodying aesthetic themes common to both.

Ironically, those values conventionally associated with white working-class culture (the values of what John Clarke (1976) calls 'the defensively organised collective') which had been eroded by time, by relative affluence and by the disruption of the physical environment in which they had been rooted, were rediscovered embedded in black West Indian culture. Here was a culture armoured against contaminating influences, protected against the more frontal assaults of the dominant ideology, denied access to the 'good life' by the colour of its skin. Its rituals, language and style provided models for those white youths alienated from the parent culture by the imagined compromises of the post-war years. The skinheads, then, resolved or at least reduced the tension between an experienced present (the mixed ghetto) and an imaginary past (the classic white slum) by initiating a dialogue which reconstituted each in terms of the other.

But this 'conversation' itself inevitably created certain problems. After all, the most conspicuous sign of change (the black presence in traditionally white working-class areas) was being used by the skinheads to re-establish continuity with a broken past, to rehabilitate a damaged integrity, to resist other less tangible changes (embourgeoisement, the myth of classlessness, the breakdown of the extended family, the substitution of private for communal space, gentrification, etc.) which threatened the structure of the traditional community at a far deeper level. Needless to say, the alliance between white and black youths was an extremely precarious and provisional one: it was only by continually monitoring trouble spots (e.g. the distribution of white girls) and by scapegoating other alien groups ('queers', hippies, and Asians) that internal conflict could be avoided. Most notably, 'paki-bashing' can be read as a displacement manoeuvre whereby the fear and anxiety produced by limited identification with one black group was transformed into aggression and directed against another black community. Less easily assimilated than the West Indians into the host community, as both Clarke (1976a, p. 102) and Cohen (1972a, pp. 29–30) take pains to point out, sharply differentiated not only by racial characteristics but by religious rituals, food taboos and a value system which encouraged deference, frugality and the profit motive, the Pakistanis were singled out for the brutal attentions of skinheads, black and white alike. Every time the boot went in, a contradiction was concealed, glossed over, made to 'disappear'.

As the 70s approached, the line between the past and the present, between black and white cultures, became increasingly difficult to hold. Ian Taylor and Dave Wall (1976) stress the further erosion of many pre-war, working-class institutions (the very institutions which the skinheads sought to resurrect), citing the 'collapse of the working class week-end', the 'bourgeoisification' of football and leisure in general, and the sensitization of 'consumer capitalism to a market available for a class-based product' (i.e. glam rock) as factors central to the decline of the skinhead subculture. In addition, there were ideological shifts inside reggae which threatened to exclude white youths. As the music became more openly committed to racial themes and

Rastafarianism, the basic contradictions began to explode onto the surfaces of life, to burst into the arena of aesthetics and style where the original truce between the two groups had been signed. As reggae became increasingly preoccupied with its own blackness, it began to appeal less and less to the skinheads who were gradually edged out at a time when the cycle of obsolescence had, as far as this particular subculture was concerned, almost run its course. Wall and Taylor (1976) mention the summer of 1972 when the skinheads joined other white residents to attack second-generation immigrants in the Toxteth area of Liverpool as a 'crucial date in the "natural history" of the skinheads'. Certainly by the early part of the decade

> ... the skinheads turned away in disbelief as they heard the Rastas sing of the 'have-nots seeking harmony' and the scatting dee-jays exhorting their black brothers to be 'good in (the) neighbourhood'. .... It must have seemed as the rudies closed their ranks that they had also changed their sides and the doors were doubly locked against the bewildered skinhead. ... Reggae had come of age and the skinheads were sentenced to perpetual adolescence. ...
> (Hebdige, 1976)

Glam and glitter rock: Albino camp and other diversions

The segregation of black British culture during the early 70s, symbolized for Wall and Taylor by the launching in November 1973 of a magazine called *Black Music* aimed specifically at the West Indian market, created a kind of impasse in white working-class youth culture. After all, I-Roy's '(It's a) Black Man Time' – extremely popular with young blacks – could scarcely be expected to appeal to white youngsters. As the finer distinctions in the Rastafarian ideology were coarsened and conveniently discarded in the passage to Britain, it became all too easy for black youths to dismiss their white contemporaries along with the teachers, the police and the bosses as 'Babylon' or 'crazy baldheads'.[14]

Left to its own devices, pop tended to atrophy into vacuous disco-bounce and sugary ballads, while 'glam' rock, representing a synthesis of two dead or dying subcultures – the Underground and the skinheads – began to pursue an exclusively white line away from soul and reggae; a line which led, according at least to Wall and Taylor, into the clutches of consumer-capitalism, towards the self-consciously European obsessions described above (pp. 27–9). Bowie, in particular, in a series of 'camp' incarnations (Ziggy Stardust, Aladdin Sane, Mr Newton, the thin white duke, and more depressingly the Blond Fuehrer) achieved something of a cult status in the early 70s. He attracted a mass youth (rather than teeny-bopper) audience and set up a number of visual precedents in terms of personal appearance (make-up, dyed hair, etc.) which created a new sexually ambiguous image for those youngsters willing and brave enough to challenge the notoriously pedestrian stereotypes conventionally available to working-class men and women. Every Bowie concert performed in drab provincial cinemas and Victorian town halls attracted a host of startling Bowie lookalikes, self-consciously cool under gangster hats which concealed (at least until the doors were opened) hair rinsed a luminous vermilion, orange, or scarlet streaked with gold and silver. These exquisite creatures, perched nervously on platform shoes or slouching (just like the Boy himself in that last publicity release) in 50s plastic sandals, cigarette held just so, shoulders set at such and such an angle, were involved in a game of make-believe which has embarrassed and appalled some commentators on the rock scene who are concerned for the 'authenticity' and oppositional content of youth culture. Taylor and Wall, for instance, are particularly incensed over Bowie's alleged 'emasculation' of the Underground tradition:

Bowie has in effect colluded in consumer capitalism's attempt to re-create a dependent adolescent class, involved as passive teenage consumers in the purchase of leisure prior to the assumption of 'adulthood' rather than being a youth culture of persons who question (from whatever class or cultural perspective) the value and meaning of adolescence and the transition to the adult world of work. (1976)

Certainly Bowie's position was devoid of any obvious political or counter-cultural significance, and those messages which were allowed to penetrate the distractive screens were, on the whole, positively objectionable ('Hitler was the first superstar. He really did it right', reported in *Temporary Hoarding*, a Rock Against Racism periodical). Not only was Bowie patently uninterested either in contemporary political and social issues or in working-class life in general, but his entire aesthetic was predicated upon a deliberate avoidance of the 'real' world and the prosaic language in which that world was habitually described, experienced and reproduced.

Bowie's meta-message was escape – from class, from sex, from personality, from obvious commitment – into a fantasy past (Isherwood's Berlin peopled by a ghostly cast of doomed bohemians) or a science-fiction future. When the contemporary 'crisis' was addressed, it was done so obliquely, represented in transmogrified form as a dead world of humanoids, ambiguously relished and reviled. As far as Bowie was concerned (and the Sex Pistols after him) there could be 'no future for you, No future for me' ('God Save the Queen', Virgin, 1977) and yet Bowie was responsible for opening up questions of sexual identity which had previously been repressed, ignored or merely hinted at in rock and youth culture. In glam rock, at least amongst those artists placed, like Bowie and Roxy Music, at the more sophisticated end of the glitter spectrum, the subversive emphasis was shifted away from class and youth onto sexuality and gender typing. Although Bowie was by no means liberated in any mainstream radical sense, preferring disguise and dandyism – what Angela Carter (1976) has described as the 'ambivalent triumph of the oppressed'[15] – to any 'genuine' transcendence of sexual role play, he and, by extension, those who copied his style, *did* 'question the value and meaning of adolescence and the transition to the adult world of work' (Taylor and Wall, 1976). And they did so in singular fashion, by artfully confounding the images of men and women through which the passage from childhood to maturity was traditionally accomplished.

Bleached roots: Punks and white ethnicity

'It reminds me of the T.V. series "Roots", seeing those chains and the dog collar round the neck.' (A punk's mother interviewed in *Woman's Own*, 15 October 1977)

'Punks are niggers.' (Richard Hell, punk musician interviewed in *New Musical Express*, 29 October 1977)

Glam rock tended to alienate the majority of working-class youth precisely because it breached such basic expectancies. By the mid-70s, the fans were divided into two distinct factions. One was composed almost entirely of teeny-boppers who followed the mainstream glitter bands (Marc Bolan, Gary Glitter, Alvin Stardust). The other, consisting of older, more self-conscious teenagers, remained fastidiously devoted to the more esoteric artists (Bowie, Lou Reed, Roxy Music) whose extreme foppishness, incipient élitism, and morbid pretensions to art and intellect effectively precluded the growth of a larger mass audience. The lyrics and life-styles of these latter groups became progressively more disengaged from the mundane concerns of everyday life and adolescence (though this discrepancy had provided the initial appeal).

The punk aesthetic, formulated in the widening gap between artist and audience, can be read as an attempt to expose glam rock's implicit contradictions. For example, the 'working classness', the scruffiness and earthiness of punk ran directly counter to the arrogance, elegance and verbosity of the glam rock superstars. However, this did not prevent the two forms from sharing a certain amount of common ground. Punk claimed to speak for the neglected constituency of white lumpen youth, but it did so typically in the stilted language of glam and glitter rock – 'rendering' working classness metaphorically in chains and hollow cheeks, 'dirty' clothing (stained jackets, tarty see-through blouses) and rough and ready diction. Resorting to parody, the blank generation, 'classified null by society' (Richard Hell, *New Musical Express*, 29 October 1977) described itself in bondage through an assortment of darkly comic signifiers – straps and chains, strait jackets and rigid postures. Despite its proletarian accents, punk's rhetoric was steeped in irony.

Punk thus represents a deliberately scrawled addendum to the 'text' of glam rock – an addendum designed to puncture glam rock's extravagantly ornate style. Punk's guttersnipe rhetoric, its obsession with class and relevance were expressly designed to undercut the intellectual posturing of the previous generation of rock musicians. This reaction in its turn directed the new wave towards reggae and the associated styles which the glam rock cult had originally excluded. Reggae attracted those punks who wished to give tangible form to their alienation. It carried the necessary conviction, the political bite, so obviously missing in most contemporary white music.

Dread, in particular, was an enviable commodity. It was the means with which to menace, and the elaborate freemasonry through which it was sustained and communicated on the street – the colours, the locks, the patois – was awesome and forbidding, suggesting as it did an impregnable solidarity, an asceticism born of suffering. The concept of dread provided a key to a whole secret language: an exotic semantic interior which was irrevocably closed against white Christian sympathies (i.e. blacks are just like us) while its very existence confirmed the worst white chauvinist fears (i.e. blacks are nothing like us).

But paradoxically it was here, in the exclusiveness of Black West Indian style, in the virtual impossibility of authentic white identification, that reggae's attraction for the punks was strongest. As we have seen, the clotted language of Rastafarianism was deliberately opaque. It had grown out of patois, and patois itself had been spoken for centuries beneath the Master's comprehension. This was a language capable of piercing the most respectfully inclined white ear, and the themes of Back to Africa and Ethiopianism, celebrated in reggae, made no concessions to the sensibilities of a white audience. Reggae's blackness was proscriptive. It was an alien essence, a foreign body which implicitly threatened mainstream British culture from within [16] and as such it resonated with punk's adopted values – 'anarchy', 'surrender' and 'decline'.

For the punks to find a positive meaning in such a blatant disavowal of Britishness amounted to a symbolic act of treason which complemented, indeed completed, the sacrilegious programme undertaken in punk rock itself (c.f. the Sex Pistols' 'Anarchy in the U.K.' and 'God Save the Queen', Jordan's rendition of 'Rule Britannia' in Derek Jarman's film *Jubilee*). The punks capitulated to alienation, losing themselves in the unfamiliar contours of an alien form. In this way, the very factors which had dictated the skinheads' withdrawal in the late 60s facilitated the punks' involvement a decade later. Just as the mod and skinhead styles had obliquely reproduced the 'cool' look and feel of the West Indian rude boys and were symbolically placed in the same ideal milieux (the Big City, the violent slum), so the punk aesthetic can be read in part as a white 'translation' of black 'ethnicity' (see pp. 42–3).

This parallel white 'ethnicity' was defined through contradictions. On the one hand it centred, however iconoclastically, on traditional notions of Britishness (the Queen, the Union Jack, etc.). It was 'local'. It emanated from the recognizable locales of Britain's inner cities. It spoke in city accents. And yet, on the other hand, it was predicated upon a denial of place. It issued out of nameless housing estates, anonymous dole queues, slums-in-the-abstract. It was blank, expressionless, rootless. In this the punk subculture can be contrasted against the West Indian styles which had provided the basic models. Whereas urban black youths could place themselves through reggae 'beyond the pale' in an imagined elsewhere (Africa, the West Indies) the punks were tied to present time. They were bound to a Britain which had no foreseeable future.

But this difference could be magically elided. By simple sleight of hand, the co-ordinates of time and place could be dissolved, transcended, converted into signs. Thus it was that the punks turned towards the world a dead white face which was there and yet not 'there'. Like the myths of Roland Barthes, these 'murdered victims' – emptied and inert – also had an alibi, an elsewhere, literally 'made up' out of vaseline and cosmetics, hair dye and mascara. But paradoxically, in the case of the punks, this 'elsewhere' was also a nowhere – a twilight zone – a zone constituted out of negativity. Like André Breton's Dada, punk might seem to 'open all the doors' but these doors 'gave onto a circular corridor' (Breton, 1937).

Once inside this desecrated circle, punk was forever condemned to act out alienation, to mime its imagined condition, to manufacture a whole series of subjective correlatives for the official archetypes of the 'crisis of modern life': the unemployment figures, the Depression, the Westway, Television, etc. Converted into icons (the safety pin, the rip, the mindless lean and hungry look) these paradigms of crisis could live a double life, at once fictional and real. They reflected in a heightened form a perceived condition: a condition of unmitigated exile, voluntarily assumed. But whereas exile had a specific meaning, implied a specific (albeit magical) solution in the context of Rastafarianism and Negro history, when applied metaphorically to British white youth it could only delineate a hopeless condition. It could neither promise a future nor explain a past. Trapped in the paradox of 'divine' subordination like Saint Genet[17] who 'chooses' the Fate which has been bestowed upon him, the punks dissembled, dying to recreate themselves in caricature, to 'dress up' their Destiny in its true colours, to substitute the diet for hunger,[18] to slide the ragamuffin look ('unkempt' but meticulously coutured) between poverty and elegance. Punk, having found an adequate reflection in the shards of broken glass, having spoken through the holes in purposefully torn tee-shirts, having brought dishonour on the family name[19], found itself again at the point from which it had started: as a 'lifer' in 'solitary' despite the fierce tattoos.

These contradictions were literally re-presented in the form of punk's association with reggae. At one level, the punks openly acknowledged the significance of contact and exchange, and on occasion even elevated the cultural connection into a political commitment. Punk groups for instance, figured prominently in the Rock against Racism campaign set up to combat the growing influence of the National Front in working-class areas.[20] But at another, deeper level, the association seems to have been repressed, displaced on the part of the punks into the construction of a music which was emphatically white and even more emphatically British.

In the event, certain features were lifted directly from the black West Indian rude and Rasta styles. For example, one of the characteristic punk hair-styles consisting of a petrified mane held in a state of vertical tension by means of vaseline, lacquer or soap, approximated to the black 'natty' or dreadlock styles. Some punks wore Ethiopian colours and the Rasta rhetoric began to work its way into the repertoires of some punk groups. The Clash and the Slits in particular wove reggae slogans and themes into their material, and in 1977 the reggae group Culture produced a song describing the impending apocalypse entitled 'When the Two Sevens Clash', which became something of a catchphrase in select punk circles. Some groups (e.g. the Clash, Alternative T.V.) incorporated reggae numbers into their sets and a new hybrid form – punk dub [21] – grew out of the liaison. From the outset, when the first punks began to congregate at the Roxy Club in London's Covent Garden, heavy reggae had occupied a privileged position inside the subculture as the only tolerated alternative to punk, providing melodic relief from the frantic *Sturm und Drang* of new wave music. Partly for reasons of expediency (i.e. in the early days there was no recorded punk music) and partly through choice (because reggae was obviously 'rebel music') the more esoteric Jamaican imports were played regularly in many punk clubs in the intervals between live acts.

The punks' open identification with black British and West Indian culture served to antagonize the teddy boy revivalists, and the ted/punk battles played out every Saturday afternoon along the King's Road in the summer of 1977 provided spectacular evidence of the fundamental tension between the two subcultures. As early as 5 July, Rockin' Mick, a 19-year-old teddy boy (fluorescent socks, black suede creepers and jacket emblazoned with the legends 'Confederate Rock' and 'Gene Vincent lives') was expressing his disgust for the punks' lack of patriotism to an *Evening Standard* reporter, adding 'We're not against the blacks, let's just say we're not with them ...' (5 July 1977).

However, despite the strong affinity, the integrity of the two forms – punk and reggae – was scrupulously maintained, and far from simulating reggae's form and timbre, punk music, like every other aspect of punk style, tended to develop in direct antithesis to its apparent sources. Reggae and punk were audibly opposed. Where punk depended on the treble, reggae relied on the bass. Where punk launched frontal assaults on the established meaning systems, reggae communicated through ellipsis and allusion. Indeed, the way in which the two forms were rigorously, almost wilfully segregated would seem to direct us towards a concealed identity, which in turn can be used to illuminate larger patterns of interaction between immigrant and host communities. To use a term from semiotics, we could say that punk includes reggae as a 'present absence' – a black hole around which punk composes itself. This can be extended metaphorically to wider issues of race and race relations. Thus we could say that the rigid demarcation of the line between punk rock and reggae is symptomatic not only of an 'identity crisis' peculiar to the punk subculture but also of those more general contradictions and tensions which inhibit the development of an open dialogue between an immigrant culture with a strong 'ethnic' character and the indigenous working-class culture which technically 'encloses' it.

We can now return to consider the meaning of that uneasy relation between rock and reggae characteristic of punk. We have seen how punk's belligerent insistence on class and relevance was at least partly determined by the ethereal excesses of the glam rock cult, and that the particular form this insistence took (the vagrant aesthetic, a singular music) was also indirectly influenced by the subcultural styles of the black immigrant community. This dialectical movement from white to black and back again is by no means solely confined to the punk subculture. On the contrary, as we have seen, the same movement is 'captured' and displayed in the styles of each of the spectacular postwar, working-class youth cultures. More particularly, it runs through rock music (and earlier, jazz) from the mid-50s onwards, dictating each successive shift in rhythm, style and

lyrical content. We are now in a position to describe this
dialectic.

As the music and the various subcultures it supports or
reproduces assume rigid and identifiable patterns, so new
subcultures are created which demand or produce corresponding mutations in musical form. These mutations in
their turn occur at those moments when forms and themes
imported from contemporary black music break up (or
'overdetermine') the existing musical structure and force its
elements into new configurations. For instance, the stabili-
zation of rock in the early 6os (vapid high school bop,
romantic ballads, gimmicky instrumentals) encouraged the
mods to migrate to soul and ska, and the subsequent re-
affirmation of black themes and rhythms by white r & b and
soul bands [22] contributed to the resurgence of rock in the
mid-6os. Similarly, at the moment when glam rock had
exhausted the permutations available within its own distinctive structure of concerns, the punks moved back to
earlier, more vigorous forms of rock (i.e. to the 5os and
mid-6os when the black influences had been strongest [23]) and
forward to contemporary reggae (dub, Bob Marley) in
order to find a music which reflected more adequately their
sense of frustration and oppression.

However, here as elsewhere in punk, the mutation seems
deliberate, constructed. Perhaps, given the differences
between them, there can be no easy synthesis of the two
languages of rock and reggae. The fundamental lack of fit
between these two languages (dress, dance, speech, music,
drugs, style, history) exposed in the emergence of black
ethnicity in reggae, generates a peculiarly unstable dynamic
within the punk subculture. This tension gave punk its
curiously petrified quality, its paralysed look, its 'dumb-
ness' which found a silent voice in the smooth moulded
surfaces of rubber and plastic, in the bondage and robotics
which signify 'punk' to the world. For, at the heart of the
punk subculture, forever arrested, lies this frozen dialectic

between black and white cultures – a dialectic which beyond a certain point (i.e. ethnicity) is incapable of renewal, trapped, as it is, within its own history, imprisoned within its own irreducible antinomies.

PART TWO:
A READING

It has become something of a cliché to talk of the period after the Second World War as one of enormous upheaval in which the traditional patterns of life in Britain were swept aside to be replaced by a new, and superficially less class-ridden system. Sociologists have dwelt in particular upon the disintegration of the working-class community[2] and have demonstrated how the demolition of the traditional environment of back-to-backs and corner shops merely signified deeper and more intangible changes. As Berger (1967) points out, landmarks are not only 'geographic but also biographical and personal', and the disappearance of the familiar landmarks after the War presaged the collapse of a whole way of life.

None the less, despite the confident assurances of both Labour and Conservative politicians that Britain was now entering a new age of unlimited affluence and equal opportunity, that we had 'never had it so good', class refused to disappear. The ways in which class was *lived*, however – the forms in which the experience of class found expression in culture – did change dramatically. The advent of the mass media, changes in the constitution of the family, in the organization of school and work, shifts in the relative status of work and leisure, all served to fragment and polarize the working-class community, producing a series of marginal discourses within the broad confines of class experience.

The development of youth culture should be seen as just part of this process of polarization. Specifically, we can cite the relative increase in the spending power of working-class youth,[3] the creation of a market designed to absorb the resulting surplus, and changes in the education system consequent upon the 1944 Butler Act as factors contributing to the emergence after the War of a generational consciousness amongst the young. This consciousness was still rooted in a generalized experience of class, but it was expressed in ways which were different from, and in some cases openly antithetical to, the traditional forms.

The persistence of class as a meaningful category within youth culture was not, however, generally acknowledged until fairly recently and, as we shall see, the seemingly spontaneous eruption of spectacular youth styles has encouraged some writers to talk of youth as the new class – to see in youth a community of undifferentiated Teenage Consumers. It was not until the 60s, when Peter Willmott (1969) and David Downes (1966) published separate pieces of research into the lives of working-class adolescents,[4] that the myth of a classless youth culture was seriously challenged. This challenge is best understood in the context of the larger debate about the function of subculture which has, for many years, preoccupied those sociologists who specialize in deviancy theory. It would seem appropriate to include here a brief survey of some of the approaches to youth and subculture put forward in the course of that debate.

The study of subculture in Britain grew out of a tradition of urban ethnography which can be traced back at least as far as the nineteenth century: to the work of Henry Mayhew and Thomas Archer,[5] and to the novels of Charles Dickens and Arthur Morrison.[6] However, a more 'scientific' approach to subculture complete with its own methodology (participant observation) did not emerge until the 1920s when a group of sociologists and criminologists in Chicago began collecting evidence on juvenile street gangs and deviant groups (professional criminals, bootleggers, etc.). In 1927, Frederick Thrasher produced a survey of over 1000 street gangs, and later William Foote Whyte described at length in *Street Corner Society* the rituals, routines and occasional exploits of one particular gang.

Participant observation continues to produce some of the most interesting and evocative accounts of subculture, but the method also suffers from a number of significant flaws. In particular, the absence of any analytical or explanatory framework has guaranteed such work a marginal status in the predominantly positivist tradition of mainstream sociology.[7] More crucially, such an absence has ensured that while accounts based upon a participant observation approach provide a wealth of descriptive detail, the significance of class and power relations is consistently neglected or at least underestimated. In such accounts, the subculture tends to be presented as an independent organism functioning outside the larger social, political and economic contexts. As a result, the picture of subculture is often incomplete. For all the Chandleresque qualities of the prose; for all the authenticity and close detail which participant observation made possible, it soon became apparent that the method needed to be supplemented by other more analytical procedures.

During the 1950s, Albert Cohen and Walter Miller sought to supply the missing theoretical perspective by tracing the continuities and breaks between dominant and subordinate value systems. Cohen stressed the compensatory function of the juvenile gang: working-class adolescents who underachieved at school joined gangs in their leisure time in order to develop alternative sources of self-esteem. In the gang, the core values of the straight world – sobriety, ambition, conformity, etc. – were replaced by their opposites: hedonism, defiance of authority and the quest for 'kicks' (Cohen, 1955). Miller, too, concentrated on the value system of the juvenile gang, but he underlined the similarities between gang and parent culture, arguing that many of the values of the deviant group merely reiterated in a distorted or heightened form the 'focal concerns' of the adult working-class population (Miller, 1958). In 1961, Matza and Sykes used the notion of subterranean values to explain the existence of legitimate as well as delinquent youth cultures. Like Miller, the writers recognized that potentially subversive goals and aims were present in systems which were otherwise regarded as perfectly respectable. They found embedded in youth culture those subterranean values (the search for risk, excitement, etc.) which served to underpin rather than undermine the day-time ethos of production (postponement of gratification, routine, etc.) (Matza and Sykes, 1961; Matza, 1964).[8]

Subsequently, these theories were tested in the course of British field work. In the 60s, Peter Willmott published his research into the range of cultural options open to working-class boys in the East End of London. Contrary to the breezy assertions of writers like Mark Abrams (1959),[9] Willmott concluded that the idea of a completely classless youth culture was premature and meaningless. He observed instead that the leisure styles available to youth were inflected through the contradictions and divisions intrinsic to a class society. It was left to Phil Cohen to explore in detail the ways in which class-specific experience was encoded in leisure styles which after all had largely originated in London's East End. Cohen was also interested in the links between youth and parent cultures, and interpreted the various youth styles as sectional adaptations to changes which had disrupted the *whole* East End community. He defined subculture as a '. . . compromise solution between two contradictory needs: the need to create and express autonomy and difference from parents . . . and the need to maintain the parental identifications' (Cohen, 1972a). In this analysis, the mod, ted and skinhead styles were interpreted as attempts to mediate between experience and tradition, the familiar and the novel. And for Cohen, the 'latent function' of subculture was to '. . . express and resolve, albeit magically, the contradictions which remain hidden or unresolved in the parent culture' (Cohen, 1972a). The mods, for instance

> . . . attempted to realise, but in an imaginary relation, the condition of existence of the socially mobile white-collar worker . . . [while] . . . their argot and ritual forms . . . [continued to stress] . . . many of the traditional values of the parent culture. (Cohen, 1972a)

Here at last was a reading which took into account the full interplay of ideological, economic and cultural factors which bear upon subculture. By grounding his theory in ethnographic detail, Cohen was able to insert class into his analysis at a far more sophisticated level than had previously been possible. Rather than presenting class as an abstract set of external determinations, he showed it working out in practice as a material force, dressed up, as it were, in experience and exhibited in style. The raw material of history could be seen refracted, held and 'handled' in the line of a mod's jacket, in the soles on a teddy boy's shoes. Anxieties concerning class and sexuality, the tensions between conformity and deviance, family and school, work and leisure, were all frozen there in a form which was at once visible and opaque, and Cohen provided a way of reconstructing that history; of penetrating the skin of style and drawing out its hidden meanings.

Cohen's work still furnishes the most adequate model available for a reading of subcultural style. However, in order to underline the importance and meaning of class, he had been forced to lay perhaps too much emphasis on the links between the youth and adult working-class cultures. There are equally significant differences between the two forms which must also be acknowledged. As we have seen, a generational consciousness *did* emerge amongst the young in the post-war period, and even where experience was shared between parents and children this experience was likely to be differently interpreted, expressed and handled by the two groups. Thus, while obviously there are points where parent and adolescent 'solutions' converge and even overlap, when dealing with the spectacular subculture we should not grant these an absolute ascendancy. And we should be careful when attempting to tie back subcultural style to its generative context not to overstress the fit between respectable working-class culture and the altogether more marginal forms with which we are concerned here.

For example, the skinheads undoubtedly reasserted those values associated with the traditional working-class community, but they did so *in the face of* the widespread renunciation of those values in the parent culture – *at a time when* such an affirmation of the classic concerns of working-class life was considered inappropriate. Similarly, the mods were negotiating changes and contradictions which were simultaneously affecting the parent culture but they were doing so in the terms of their own relatively autonomous problematic – by inventing an 'elsewhere' (the week-end, the West End) which was defined *against* the familiar locales of the home, the pub, the working-man's club, the neighbourhood (see p. 53).

If we emphasize integration and coherence at the expense of dissonance and discontinuity, we are in danger of denying the very manner in which the subcultural form is made to crystallize, objectify and communicate group experience. We should be hard pressed to find in the punk subculture, for instance, any symbolic attempts to 'retrieve some of the socially cohesive elements destroyed in the parent culture' (Cohen, 1972a) beyond the simple fact of cohesion itself: the expression of a highly structured, visible, tightly bounded group identity. Rather, the punks seemed to be parodying the alienation and emptiness which have caused sociologists so much concern,[10] realizing in a deliberate and wilful fashion the direst predictions of the most scathing social critics, and celebrating in mock-heroic terms the death of the community and the collapse of traditional forms of meaning.

We can, therefore, only grant a qualified acceptance to Cohen's theory of subcultural style. Later, I shall be attempting to re-think the relationship between parent and youth cultures by looking more closely at the whole process of signification in subculture. At this stage, however, we should not allow these objections to detract from the overall importance of Cohen's contribution. It is no exaggeration to say that the idea of style as a coded response to changes affecting the entire community has literally transformed the study of spectacular youth culture. Much of the research extracted in *Resistance Through Rituals* (Hall *et al*. 1976a) was premised upon the basic assumption that style could be read in this way. Using Gramsci's concept of hegemony (see pp. 15–19), the authors interpreted the succession of youth cultural styles as symbolic forms of resistance; as spectacular symptoms of a wider and more generally submerged dissent which characterized the whole post-war period. This reading of style opens up a number of issues which demand examination, and the approach to subculture adopted in *Resistance Through Rituals* provides the basis for much of what follows. We begin with the notion of specificity.

Specificity: Two types of teddy boy

If we take as our starting point the definition of culture used in *Resistance Through Rituals* – culture is '. . . that level at which social groups develop distinct patterns of life and give *expressive form* to their social and material . . . experience' (Hall *et al*., 1976a) we can see that each subculture represents a different handling of the 'raw material of social . . . existence' (Hall *et al*., 1976a). But what exactly is this 'raw material'? We learn from Marx that 'Men make their own history, but they do not make it just as they please, they do not make it under circumstances chosen by themselves, but under circumstances directly encountered, given and transmitted from the past' (Marx, 1951). In effect, the material (i.e. social relations) which is continually being transformed into culture (and hence subculture) can never be completely 'raw'. It is always mediated: inflected by the historical context in which it is encountered; posited upon a specific ideological field which gives it a particular life and particular meanings. Unless one is prepared to use some essentialist paradigm of the working class as the inexorable bearers of an absolute trans-historical Truth,[11] then one should not expect the subcultural response to be either unfailingly correct about real relations under capitalism, or even *necessarily* in touch, in any immediate sense, with its material position in the capitalist system. Spectacular subcultures express what is by definition an imaginary set of relations (see pp. 77–8). The raw material out of which they are constructed is both real and ideological. It is mediated to the individual members of a subculture through a variety of channels: school, the family, work, the media, etc. Moreover, this material is subject to historical change. Each subcultural 'instance' represents a 'solution' to a specific set of circumstances, to particular problems and contradictions. For example, the mod and teddy boy 'solutions' were produced in response to different conjunctures which positioned them differently in relation to existing cultural formations (immigrant cultures, the parent culture, other subcultures, the dominant culture). We can see this more clearly if we concentrate on one example.

There were two major moments in the history of the teddy boy subculture (the 1950s and the 1970s). But, whilst they maintained the same antagonistic relation to the black immigrant community as their counterparts of the 50s, (see pp. 50–1,) the latter-day teds were differently positioned in relation to the parent culture and other youth cultures.

The early 1950s and late 1970s share certain obvious features: the vocabularies of 'austerity' and 'crisis', though not identical, are similar, and more importantly, anxieties about the effects of black immigration on employment, housing and the 'quality of life' were prominent in both periods. However, the differences are far more crucial. The presence in the latter period of an alternative, predominantly working-class youth culture (i.e. the punks), many of whose members actively championed certain aspects of West Indian life, serve clearly to distinguish the two moments.

The early teds had marked a new departure. They had represented, in the words of George Melly (1972), 'the dark van of pop culture' and though small in number, they had been almost universally vilified by press and parents alike as symptomatic of Britain's impending decline. On the other hand, the very concept of 'revival' in the 1970s gave the teddy boys an air of legitimacy. After all, in a society which seemed to generate a bewildering number of fads and fashions, the teddy boys were a virtual institution: an authentic, albeit dubious part of the British heritage.

The youths who took part in this revival were thus guaranteed in certain quarters at least a limited acceptability. They could be regarded with tolerance, even muted affection, by those working-class adults who, whether original teds or straights, nostalgically inclined towards the 1950s and, possessed of patchy memories, harked back to a more settled and straightforward past. The revival recalled a time which seemed surprizingly remote, and by comparison secure; almost idyllic in its stolid puritanism, its sense of values, its conviction that the future could be better. Freed from time and context, these latter-day teds could be allowed to float as innocent pretenders on the wave of 1970s nostalgia situated somewhere between the Fonz of television's *Happy Days* and a recycled Ovaltine ad. Paradoxically then, the subculture which had originally furnished such dramatic signs of change could be made to provide a kind of continuity in its revived form.

In broader terms, the two teddy boy solutions were responses to specific historical conditions, formulated in completely different ideological atmospheres. There was no possibility in the late 1970s of enlisting working-class support around the cheery imperatives of reconstruction: 'grin and bear it', 'wait and see', etc. The widespread disillusionment amongst working-class people with the Labour Party and Parliamentary politics in general, the decline of the Welfare State, the faltering economy, the continuing scarcity of jobs and adequate housing, the loss of community, the failure of consumerism to satisfy real needs, and the perennial round of industrial disputes, shutdowns and picket line clashes, all served to create a sense of diminishing returns which stood in stark contrast to the embattled optimism of the earlier period. Assisted no doubt by the ideological constructions retrospectively placed upon the Second World War (the fostering around 1973 as a response to protracted industrial disputes, the oil crisis, the three day week, etc. of a patriotic war-time spirit in search of an enemy; the replacement of the concretization 'German' for the concept 'fascist') these developments further combined with the visibility of the black communities to make racism a far more respectable and credible solution to the problems of working-class life.

In addition, the teddy boys' dress and demeanour carried rather different connotations in the 1970s. Of course the 'theft' of an upper-class style which had originally made the whole teddy boy style possible had long been forgotten, and in the process the precise nature of the transformation had been irrevocably lost. What is more the strutting manner and sexual aggressiveness had different meanings in the two periods. The narcissism of the early teds and the carnal gymnastics of jiving had been pitted against what Melly (1972) describes as a 'grey colourless world where good boys played ping pong'. The second generation teds' obstinate fidelity to the traditional 'bad-guy' stereotypes appeared by contrast obvious and reactionary. To the sound of records long since deleted, in clothes which qualified as virtual museum pieces, these latter-day teds resurrected a set of sexual mores (gallantry, courtship,) and a swaggering machismo – that 'quaint' combination of chauvinism, brylcreem and sudden violence – which was already enshrined in the parent culture as *the* model of masculine behaviour: a model untouched by the febrile excesses of the post-war 'permissive society'.

All these factors drew the teddy boy subculture in its second incarnation *closer* to the parent culture and helped to define it against other existing youth cultural options (punks, Northern soul enthusiasts, heavy metal rockers,[12] football fans, mainstream pop, 'respectable', etc.) For these reasons, wearing a drape coat in 1978 did not mean the same things in the same way as it had done in 1956, despite the fact that the two sets of teddy boys worshipped identical heroes (Elvis, Eddie Cochrane, James Dean), cultivated the same quiffs and occupied approximately the same class position. The twin concepts of *conjuncture* and *specificity* (each subculture representing a distinctive 'moment' – a particular response to a particular set of circumstances) are therefore indispensable to a study of subcultural style.

The sources of style

We have seen how the experience encoded in subcultures is shaped in a variety of locales (work, home, school, etc.). Each of these locales imposes its own unique structure, its own rules and meanings, its own hierarchy of values. Though these structures articulate together, they do so syntactically. They are bound together as much through difference (home v. school, school v. work, home v. work, private v. public, etc.) as through similarity. To use Althusser's admittedly cumbersome terms, they constitute different levels of the same social formation. And though they are, as Althusser takes pains to point out, 'relatively autonomous', these structures remain, in capitalist societies, articulated around the 'general contradiction' between Capital and Labour (see particularly Althusser 1971a). The complex interplay between the different levels of the social formation is reproduced in the experience of both dominant and subordinate groups, and this experience, in turn, becomes the 'raw material' which finds expressive form in culture and subculture. Now, the media play a crucial role in defining our experience for us. They provide us with the most available categories for classifying out the social world. It is primarily through the press, television, film, etc. that experience is organized, interpreted, and made to *cohere in contradiction* as it were. It should hardly surprise us then, to discover that much of what finds itself encoded in subculture has already been subjected to a certain amount of prior handling by the media.

Thus, in post-war Britain, the loaded content of subcultural style is likely to be as much a function of what Stuart Hall has called the 'ideological effect'[13] of the media as a reaction to experienced changes in the institutional framework of working-class life. As Hall has argued, the media have 'progressively colonised the cultural and ideological sphere':

> As social groups and classes live, if not in their productive then in their 'social' relations, increasingly fragmented and sectionally differentiated lives, the mass media are more and more responsible (a) for providing the basis on which groups and classes construct an image of the lives, meanings, practices and values of *other* groups and classes; (b) for providing the images, representations and ideas around which the social totality composed of all these separate and fragmented pieces can be coherently grasped. (Hall, 1977)

So a credible image of social cohesion can only be maintained through the appropriation and redefinition of cultures of resistance (e.g. working-class youth cultures) in terms of that image. In this way, the media not only provide groups with substantive images of other groups, they also relay back to working-class people a 'picture' of their own lives which is 'contained' or 'framed' by the ideological discourses which surround and situate it.

Clearly, subcultures are not privileged forms; they do not

stand outside the reflexive circuitry of production and reproduction which links together, at least on a symbolic level, the separate and fragmented pieces of the social totality. Subcultures are, at least in part, representations of these representations, and elements taken from the 'picture' of working-class life (and of the social whole in general) are bound to find some echo in the signifying practices of the various subcultures. There is no reason to suppose that subcultures spontaneously affirm only those *blocked* 'readings' excluded from the airwaves and the newspapers (consciousness of subordinate status, a conflict model of society, etc.). They also articulate, to a greater or lesser extent, some of the *preferred* meanings and interpretations, those favoured by and transmitted through the authorized channels of mass communication. The typical members of a working-class youth culture in part contest and in part agree with the dominant definitions of who and what they are, and there is a substantial amount of shared ideological ground not only between them and the adult working-class culture (with its muted tradition of resistance) but also between them and the dominant culture (at least in its more 'democratic', accessible forms).

For example, the elaboration of upward and downward options open to working-class youth does not necessarily indicate any significant difference in the relative status of the jobs available to the average mod of 1964 and the skinhead of 1968 (though a census might indeed reveal such a difference). Still less does it reflect *directly* the fact that job opportunities open to working-class youth in general actually diminished during the intervening period. Rather the different styles and the ideologies which structure and determine them represent negotiated responses to a contradictory mythology of class. In this mythology, 'the withering away of class' is paradoxically countered by an undiluted 'classfulness', a romantic conception of the traditional whole way of (working-class) life revived twice weekly on television programmes like *Coronation Street*. The mods and skinheads, then, in their different ways, were 'handling' this mythology as much as the exigencies of their material condition. They were learning to live within or without that amorphous body of images and typifications made available in the mass media in which class is alternately overlooked and overstated, denied and reduced to caricature.

In the same way, the punks were not only directly *responding* to increasing joblessness, changing moral standards, the rediscovery of poverty, the Depression, etc., they were *dramatizing* what had come to be called 'Britain's decline' by constructing a language which was, in contrast to the prevailing rhetoric of the Rock Establishment, unmistakably relevant and down to earth (hence the swearing, the references to 'fat hippies', the rags, the lumpen poses). The punks appropriated the rhetoric of crisis which had filled the airwaves and the editorials throughout the period and translated it into tangible (and visible) terms. In the gloomy, apocalyptic ambience of the late 1970s – with massive unemployment, with the ominous violence of the Notting Hill Carnival, Grunwick, Lewisham and Ladywood – it was fitting that the punks should present themselves as 'degenerates'; as signs of the highly publicized decay which perfectly represented the atrophied condition of Great Britain. The various stylistic ensembles adopted by the punks were undoubtedly expressive of genuine aggression, frustration and anxiety. But these statements, no matter how strangely constructed, were cast in a language which was generally available – a language which was current. This accounts, first, for the appropriateness of the punk metaphor for both the members of the subculture and its opponents and, second, for the success of the punk subculture as spectacle: its ability to symptomatize a whole cluster of contemporary problems. It explains the subculture's ability to attract new members and to produce the requisite outraged responses from the parents, teachers and employers towards whom the moral panic was directed and from the 'moral entrepreneurs' – the local councillors, the pundits and M.P.s – who were responsible for conducting the 'crusade' against it. In order to communicate disorder, the appropriate language must first be selected, even if it is to be subverted. For punk to be dismissed as chaos, it had first to 'make sense' as noise.

We can now begin to understand how the Bowie cult came to be articulated around questions of gender rather than class, and to confront those critics who relate the legitimate concerns of 'authentic' working-class culture exclusively to the sphere of production. The Bowie-ites were certainly not grappling in any *direct* way with the familiar set of problems encountered on the shop floor and in the classroom: problems which revolve around relations with authority (rebellion v. deference, upward v. downward options, etc.). None the less, they were attempting to negotiate a meaningful intermediate space somewhere between the parent culture and the dominant ideology: a space where an alternative identity could be discovered and expressed. To this extent they were engaged in that distinctive quest for a measure of autonomy which characterizes all youth sub- (and counter) cultures (see p. 148, n. 6). In sharp contrast to their skinhead predecessors, the Bowie-ites were confronting the more obvious chauvinisms (sexual, class, territorial) and seeking, with greater or lesser enthusiasm, to avoid, subvert or overthrow them. They were simultaneously (1) challenging the traditional working-class puritanism so firmly embedded in the parent culture, (2) resisting the way in which this puritanism was being made to signify the working class in the media and (3) adapting images, styles and ideologies made available elsewhere on television and in films (e.g. the nostalgia cult of the early 1970s), in magazines and newspapers (high fashion, the emergence of feminism in its commodity form, e.g. *Cosmopolitan*) in order to construct an alternative identity which communicated a perceived difference: an Otherness. They were, in short, challenging at a symbolic level the 'inevitability', the 'naturalness' of class and gender stereotypes.

SIX

Subculture: The unnatural break

'I felt unclean for about 48 hours.' (G.L.C. councillor after seeing a concert by the Sex Pistols (reported *New Musical Express*, 18 July 1977))

[Language is] of all social institutions, the least amenable to initiative. It blends with the life of society, and the latter, inert by nature, is a prime conservative force. (Saussure, 1974)

SUBCULTURES represent 'noise' (as opposed to sound): interference in the orderly sequence which leads from real events and phenomena to their representation in the media. We should therefore not underestimate the signifying power of the spectacular subculture not only as a metaphor for potential anarchy 'out there' but as an actual mechanism of semantic disorder: a kind of temporary blockage in the system of representation. As John Mepham (1972) has written:

Distinctions and identities may be so deeply embedded in our discourse and thought about the world whether this be because of their role in our practical lives, or because they are cognitively powerful and are an important aspect of the way in which we appear to make sense of our experience, that the theoretical challenge to them can be quite startling.

Any elision, truncation or convergence of prevailing linguistic and ideological categories can have profoundly disorienting effects. These deviations briefly expose the arbitrary nature of the codes which underlie and shape all forms of discourse. As Stuart Hall (1974) has written (here in the context of explicitly political deviance):

New . . . developments which are both dramatic and 'meaningless' within the consensually validated norms, pose a challenge to the normative world. They render problematic not only how the . . . world is defined, but how it ought to be. They 'breach our expectancies'. . . .

Notions concerning the sanctity of language are intimately bound up with ideas of social order. The limits of acceptable linguistic expression are prescribed by a number of apparently universal taboos. These taboos guarantee the continuing 'transparency' (the taken-for-grantedness) of meaning.

Predictably then, violations of the authorized codes through which the social world is organized and experienced have considerable power to provoke and disturb. They are generally condemned, in Mary Douglas' words (1967), as 'contrary to holiness' and Levi-Strauss has noted how, in certain primitive myths, the mispronunciation of words and the misuse of language are classified along with incest as horrendous aberrations capable of 'unleashing storm and tempest' (Levi-Strauss, 1969). Similarly, spectacular subcultures express forbidden contents (consciousness of class, consciousness of difference) in forbidden forms (transgressions of sartorial and behavioural codes, law breaking, etc.). They are profane articulations, and they are often and significantly defined as 'unnatural'. The terms used in the tabloid press to describe those youngsters who, in their conduct or clothing, proclaim subcultural membership ('freaks', 'animals . . . who find courage, like rats, in hunting in packs'[1]) would seem to suggest that the most primitive anxieties concerning the sacred distinction between nature and culture can be summoned up by the emergence of such a group. No doubt, the breaking of rules is confused with the 'absence of rules' which, according to Levi-Strauss (1969), 'seems to provide the surest criteria for distinguishing a natural from a cultural process'. Certainly, the official reaction to the punk subculture, particularly to the Sex Pistols' use of 'foul language' on television[2] and record[3], and to the vomiting and spitting incidents at Heathrow Airport[4] would seem to indicate that these basic taboos are no less deeply sedimented in contemporary British society.

Two forms of incorporation

> Has not this society, glutted with aestheticism, already integrated former romanticisms, surrealism, existentialism and even Marxism to a point? It has, indeed, through trade, in the form of commodities. That which yesterday was reviled today becomes cultural consumer-goods, consumption thus engulfs what was intended to give meaning and direction. (Lefebvre, 1971)

We have seen how subcultures 'breach our expectancies', how they represent symbolic challenges to a symbolic order. But can subcultures always be effectively incorporated and if so, how? The emergence of a spectacular subculture is invariably accompanied by a wave of hysteria in the press. This hysteria is typically ambivalent: it fluctuates between dread and fascination, outrage and amusement. Shock and horror headlines dominate the front page (e.g. 'Rotten Razored', *Daily Mirror*, 28 June 1977) while, inside, the editorials positively bristle with 'serious' commentary[5] and the centrespreads or supplements contain delirious accounts of the latest fads and rituals (see, for example, *Observer* colour supplements 30 January, 10 July 1977, 12 February 1978). Style in particular provokes a double response: it is alternately celebrated (in the fashion page) and ridiculed or reviled (in those articles which define subcultures as social problems).

In most cases, it is the subculture's stylistic innovations which first attract the media's attention. Subsequently deviant or 'anti-social' acts – vandalism, swearing, fighting, 'animal behaviour' – are 'discovered' by the police, the judiciary, the press; and these acts are used to 'explain' the subculture's original transgression of sartorial codes. In fact, either deviant behaviour or the identification of a distinctive uniform (or more typically a combination of the two) can provide the catalyst for a moral panic. In the case of the punks, the media's sighting of punk style virtually coincided with the discovery or invention of punk deviance. The *Daily Mirror* ran its first series of alarmist centrespreads on the subculture, concentrating on the bizarre clothing and jewellery during the week (29 Nov–3 Dec 1977) in which the Sex Pistols exploded into the public eye on the Thames *Today* programme. On the other hand, the mods, perhaps because of the muted character of their style, were not identified as a group until the Bank Holiday clashes of 1964, although the subculture was, by then, fully developed, at least in London. Whichever item opens the amplifying sequence, it invariably ends with the simultaneous diffusion and defusion of the subcultural style.

As the subculture begins to strike its own eminently marketable pose, as its vocabulary (both visual and verbal) becomes more and more familiar, so the referential context to which it can be most conveniently assigned is made increasingly apparent. Eventually, the mods, the punks, the glitter rockers can be incorporated, brought back into line, located on the preferred 'map of problematic social reality' (Geertz, 1964) at the point where boys in lipstick are 'just kids dressing up', where girls in rubber dresses are 'daughters just like yours' (see pp. 98–9; 158–9, n. 8). The media, as Stuart Hall (1977) has argued, not only record resistance, they 'situate it within the dominant framework of meanings' and those young people who choose to inhabit a spectacular youth culture are simultaneously *returned*, as they are represented on T.V. and in the newspapers, to the place where common sense would have them fit (as 'animals' certainly, but also 'in the family', 'out of work', 'up to date', etc.). It is through this continual process of recuperation that the fractured order is repaired and the subculture incorporated as a diverting spectacle within the dominant mythology from which it in part emanates: as 'folk devil', as Other, as Enemy. The process of recuperation takes two characteristic forms:

(1) the conversion of subcultural signs (dress, music, etc.) into mass-produced objects (i.e. the commodity form);
(2) the 'labelling' and re-definition of deviant behaviour by dominant groups – the police, the media, the judiciary (i.e. the ideological form).

The commodity form

The first has been comprehensively handled by both journalists and academics. The relationship between the spectacular subculture and the various industries which service and exploit it is notoriously ambiguous. After all, such a subculture is concerned first and foremost with consumption. It operates exclusively in the leisure sphere ('I wouldn't wear my punk outfit for work – there's a time and a place for everything' (see note 8)). It communicates through commodities even if the meanings attached to those commodities are purposefully distorted or overthrown. It is therefore difficult in this case to maintain any absolute distinction between commercial exploitation on the one hand and creativity/originality on the other, even though these categories are emphatically opposed in the value systems of most subcultures. Indeed, the creation and diffusion of new styles is inextricably bound up with the process of production, publicity and packaging which must inevitably lead to the defusion of the subculture's subversive power – both mod and punk innovations fed back directly into high fashion and mainstream fashion. Each new subculture establishes new trends, generates new looks and sounds which feed back into the appropriate industries. As John Clarke (1976b) has observed:

> The diffusion of youth styles from the subcultures to the fashion market is not simply a 'cultural process', but a real network or infrastructure of new kinds of commercial and economic institutions. The small-scale record shops, recording companies, the boutiques and one- or two-woman manufacturing companies – these versions of artisan capitalism, rather than more generalised and unspecific phenomena, situate the dialectic of commercial 'manipulation'.

However, it would be mistaken to insist on the absolute autonomy of 'cultural' and commercial processes. As Lefebvre (1971) puts it: 'Trade is . . . both a social and an intellectual phenomenon', and commodities arrive at the market-place already laden with significance. They are, in Marx's words (1970), 'social hieroglyphs'[6] and their meanings are inflected by conventional usage.

Thus, as soon as the original innovations which signify 'subculture' are translated into commodities and made generally available, they become 'frozen'. Once removed from their private contexts by the small entrepreneurs and big fashion interests who produce them on a mass scale, they become codified, made comprehensible, rendered at once public property and profitable merchandise. In this way, the two forms of incorporation (the semantic/ideological and the 'real'/commercial) can be said to converge on the commodity form. Youth cultural styles may begin by issuing symbolic challenges, but they must inevitably end by establishing new sets of conventions; by creating new commodities, new industries or rejuvenating old ones (think of the boost punk must have given haberdashery!). This occurs irrespective of the subculture's political orientation: the macrobiotic restaurants, craft shops and 'antique markets' of the hippie era were easily converted into punk boutiques and record shops. It also happens irrespective of the startling content of the style: punk clothing and insignia could be bought mail-order by the summer of 1977, and in September of that year *Cosmopolitan* ran a review of Zandra Rhodes' latest collection of couture follies which consisted entirely of variations on the punk theme. Models smouldered beneath mountains of safety pins and plastic (the pins were jewelled, the 'plastic' wet-look satin) and the accompanying article ended with an aphorism – 'To shock is chic' – which presaged the subculture's imminent demise.

The ideological form

The second form of incorporation – the ideological – has been most adequately treated by those sociologists who operate a transactional model of deviant behaviour. For example, Stan Cohen has described in detail how one particular moral panic (surrounding the mod–rocker conflict of the mid-6os) was launched and sustained.[7] Although this type of analysis can often provide an extremely sophisticated explanation of why spectacular subcultures consistently provoke such hysterical outbursts, it tends to overlook the subtler mechanisms through which potentially threatening phenomena are handled and contained. As the use of the term 'folk devil' suggests, rather too much weight tends to be given to the sensational excesses of the tabloid press at the expense of the ambiguous reactions which are, after all, more typical. As we have seen, the way in which subcultures are represented in the media makes them both more *and less* exotic than they actually are. They are seen to contain both dangerous aliens and boisterous kids, wild animals and wayward pets. Roland Barthes furnishes a key to this paradox in his description of 'identification' – one of the seven rhetorical figures which, according to Barthes, distinguish the meta-language of bourgeois mythology. He characterizes the petit-bourgeois as a person '. . . unable to imagine the Other . . . the Other is a scandal which threatens his existence' (Barthes, 1972).

Two basic strategies have been evolved for dealing with this threat. First, the Other can be trivialized, naturalized, domesticated. Here, the difference is simply denied ('Otherness is reduced to sameness'). Alternatively, the Other can be transformed into meaningless exotica, a 'pure object, a spectacle, a clown' (Barthes, 1972). In this case, the difference is consigned to a place beyond analysis. Spectacular subcultures are continually being defined in precisely these terms. Soccer hooligans, for example, are typically placed beyond 'the bounds of common decency' and are classified as 'animals'. ('These people aren't human beings', football club manager quoted on the *News at Ten*, Sunday, 12 March 1977.) (See Stuart Hall's treatment of the press coverage of football hooligans in *Football Hooliganism* (edited by Roger Ingham, 1978).) On the other hand, the punks tended to be resituated by the press in the family, perhaps because members of the subculture deliberately obscured their origins, refused the family and willingly played the part of folk devil, presenting themselves as pure objects, as villainous clowns. Certainly, like every other youth culture, punk was perceived as a threat to the family. Occasionally this threat was represented in literal terms. For example, the *Daily Mirror* (1 August 1977) carried a photograph of a child lying in the road after a punk–ted confrontation under the headline 'VICTIM OF THE PUNK ROCK PUNCH-UP: THE BOY WHO FELL FOUL OF THE MOB'. In this case, punk's threat to the family was made 'real' (that could be my child!) through the ideological framing of photographic evidence which is popularly regarded as unproblematic.

None the less, on other occasions, the opposite line was taken. For whatever reason, the inevitable glut of articles gleefully denouncing the latest punk outrage was counterbalanced by an equal number of items devoted to the small details of punk family life. For instance, the 15 October 1977 issue of *Woman's Own* carried an article entitled 'Punks and Mothers' which stressed the classless, fancy dress aspects of punk.[8] Photographs depicting punks with smiling mothers, reclining next to the family pool, playing with the family dog, were placed above a text which dwelt on the ordinariness of individual punks: 'It's not as rocky horror as it appears' . . . 'punk can be a family affair' . . . 'punks as it happens are non-political', and, most insidiously, albeit accurately, 'Johnny Rotten is as big a household name as Hughie Green'. Throughout the summer of 1977, the *People* and the *News of the World* ran items on punk babies, punk brothers, and punk–ted weddings. All these articles served to minimize the Otherness so stridently proclaimed in punk style, and defined the subculture in precisely those terms which it sought most vehemently to resist and deny.

Once again, we should avoid making any absolute distinction between the ideological and commercial 'manipulations' of subculture. The symbolic restoration of daughters to the family, of deviants to the fold, was undertaken at a time when the widespread 'capitulation' of punk musicians to market forces was being used throughout the media to illustrate the fact that punks were 'only human after all'. The music papers were filled with the familiar success stories describing the route from rags to rags and riches – of punk musicians flying to America, of bank clerks become magazine editors or record producers, of harrassed seamstresses turned overnight into successful business women. Of course, these success stories had ambiguous implications. As with every other 'youth revolution' (e.g. the beat boom, the mod explosion and the Swinging Sixties) the relative success of a few individuals created an impression of energy, expansion and limitless upward mobility. This ultimately reinforced the image of the open society which the very presence of the punk subculture – with its rhetorical emphasis on unemployment, high-rise living and narrow options – had originally contradicted. As Barthes (1972) has written: 'myth can always, as a last resort, signify the resistance which is brought to bear against it' and it does so typically by imposing its own ideological terms, by substituting in this case 'the fairy tale of the artist's creativity'[9] for an art form 'within the compass of every consciousness',[10] a 'music' to be judged, dismissed or marketed for 'noise' – a logically consistent, self-constituted chaos. It does so finally by replacing a subculture engendered by history, a product of real historical contradictions, with a handful of brilliant nonconformists, satanic geniuses who, to use the words of Sir John Read, Chairman of E.M.I. 'become in the fullness of time, wholly acceptable and can contribute greatly to the development of modern music'.[11]

SEVEN

Style as intentional communication

I speak through my clothes. (Eco, 1973)

THE cycle leading from opposition to defusion, from resistance to incorporation encloses each successive subculture. We have seen how the media and the market fit into this cycle. We must now turn to the subculture itself to consider exactly how and what subcultural style communicates. Two questions must be asked which together present us with something of a paradox: how does a subculture make sense to its members? How is it made to signify disorder? To answer these questions we must define the meaning of style more precisely.

In 'The Rhetoric of the Image', Roland Barthes contrasts the 'intentional' advertising image with the apparently 'innocent' news photograph. Both are complex articulations of specific codes and practices, but the news photo appears more 'natural' and transparent than the advertisement. He writes – 'the signification of the image is certainly intentional . . . the advertising image is clear, or at least emphatic'. Barthes' distinction can be used analogously to point up the difference between subcultural and 'normal' styles. The subcultural stylistic ensembles – those emphatic combinations of dress, dance, argot, music, etc. – bear approximately the same relation to the more conventional formulae ('normal' suits and ties, casual wear, twin-sets, etc.) that the advertising image bears to the less consciously constructed news photograph.

Of course, signification need not be intentional, as semioticians have repeatedly pointed out. Umberto Eco writes 'not only the expressly intended communicative object . . . but every object may be viewed . . . as a sign' (Eco, 1973). For instance, the conventional outfits worn by the average man and woman in the street are chosen within the constraints of finance, 'taste', preference, etc. and these choices are undoubtedly significant. Each ensemble has its place in an internal system of differences – the conventional modes of sartorial discourse – which fit a corresponding set of socially prescribed roles and options.[1] These choices contain a whole range of messages which are transmitted through the finely graded distinctions of a number of interlocking sets – class and status, self-image and attractiveness, etc. Ultimately, if nothing else, they are expressive of 'normality' as opposed to 'deviance' (i.e. they are distinguished by their relative invisibility, their appropriateness, their 'naturalness'). However, the intentional communication is of a different order. It stands apart – a visible construction, a loaded choice. It directs attention to itself; it gives itself to be read.

This is what distinguishes the visual ensembles of spectacular subcultures from those favoured in the surrounding culture(s). They are *obviously* fabricated (even the mods, precariously placed between the worlds of the straight and the deviant, finally declared themselves different when they gathered in groups outside dance halls and on sea fronts). They *display* their own codes (e.g. the punk's ripped T-shirt) or at least demonstrate that codes are there to be used and abused (e.g. they have been thought about rather than thrown together). In this they go against the grain of

a mainstream culture whose principal defining characteristic, according to Barthes, is a tendency to masquerade
as nature, to substitute 'normalized' for historical forms, to
translate the reality of the world into an image of the world
which in turn presents itself as if composed according to 'the
evident laws of the natural order' (Barthes, 1972).

As we have seen, it is in this sense that subcultures can be
said to transgress the laws of 'man's second nature'.[2] By
repositioning and recontextualizing commodities, by subverting their conventional uses and inventing new ones, the
subcultural stylist gives the lie to what Althusser has called
the 'false obviousness of everyday practice' (Althusser and
Balibar, 1968), and opens up the world of objects to new and
covertly oppositional readings. The communication of a
significant *difference*, then (and the parallel communication
of a group *identity*), is the 'point' behind the style of all
spectacular subcultures. It is the superordinate term under
which all the other significations are marshalled, the message
through which all the other messages speak. Once we have
granted this initial difference a primary determination over
the whole sequence of stylistic generation and diffusion, we
can go back to examine the internal structure of individual
subcultures. To return to our earlier analogy: if the spectacular subculture is an intentional communication, if it is,
to borrow a term from linguistics, 'motivated', what precisely is being communicated and advertised?

Style as *bricolage*

> It is conventional to call 'monster' any blending of disso-
> nant elements. . . . I call 'monster' every original, in-
> exhaustible beauty. (Alfred Jarry)

The subcultures with which we have been dealing share a
common feature apart from the fact that they are all predominantly working class. They are, as we have seen,

cultures of conspicuous consumption – even when, as with the skinheads and the punks, certain types of consumption are conspicuously refused – and it is through the distinctive rituals of consumption, through style, that the subculture at once reveals its 'secret' identity and communicates its forbidden meanings. It is basically the way in which commodities are *used* in subculture which mark the subculture off from more orthodox cultural formations.

Discoveries made in the field of anthropology are helpful here. In particular, the concept of *bricolage* can be used to explain how subcultural styles are constructed. In *The Savage Mind* Levi-Strauss shows how the magical modes utilized by primitive peoples (superstition, sorcery, myth) can be seen as implicitly coherent, though explicitly bewildering, systems of connection between things which perfectly equip their users to 'think' their own world. These magical systems of connection have a common feature: they are capable of infinite extension because basic elements can be used in a variety of improvised combinations to generate new meanings within them. *Bricolage* has thus been described as a 'science of the concrete' in a recent definition which clarifies the original anthropological meaning of the term:

[Bricolage] refers to the means by which the non-literate, non-technical mind of so-called 'primitive' man responds to the world around him. The process involves a 'science of the concrete' (as opposed to our 'civilised' science of the 'abstract') which far from lacking logic, in fact carefully and precisely orders, classifies and arranges into structures the *minutiae* of the physical world in all their profusion by means of a 'logic' which is not our own. The structures, 'improvised' or made up (these are rough translations of the process of *bricoler*) as *ad hoc* responses to an environment, then serve to establish homologies and analogies between the ordering of nature and that of society, and so satisfactorily 'explain' the world and make it able to be lived in. (Hawkes, 1977)

The implications of the structured improvisations of *bricolage* for a theory of spectacular subculture as a system of communication have already been explored. For instance, John Clarke has stressed the way in which prominent forms of discourse (particularly fashion) are radically adapted, subverted and extended by the subcultural *bricoleur*:

> Together, object and meaning constitute a sign, and, within any one culture, such signs are assembled, repeatedly, into characteristic forms of discourse. However, when the bricoleur re-locates the significant object in a different position within that discourse, using the same overall repertoire of signs, or when that object is placed within a different total ensemble, a new discourse is constituted, a different message conveyed. (Clarke, 1976)

In this way the teddy boy's theft and transformation of the Edwardian style revived in the early 1950s by Savile Row for wealthy young men about town can be construed as an act of *bricolage*. Similarly, the mods could be said to be functioning as *bricoleurs* when they appropriated another range of commodities by placing them in a symbolic ensemble which served to erase or subvert their original straight meanings. Thus pills medically prescribed for the treatment of neuroses were used as ends-in-themselves, and the motor scooter, originally an ultra-respectable means of transport, was turned into a menacing symbol of group solidarity. In the same improvisatory manner, metal combs, honed to a razor-like sharpness, turned narcissism into an offensive weapon. Union jacks were emblazoned on the backs of grubby parka anoraks or cut up and converted into smartly tailored jackets. More subtly, the conventional insignia of the business world – the suit, collar and tie, short hair, etc. – were stripped of their original connotations – efficiency, ambition, compliance with authority – and transformed into 'empty' fetishes, objects to be desired, fondled and valued in their own right.

At the risk of sounding melodramatic, we could use Umberto Eco's phrase 'semiotic guerilla warfare' (Eco, 1972) to describe these subversive practices. The war may be conducted at a level beneath the consciousness of the individual members of a spectacular subculture (though the subculture is still, at another level, an intentional communication (see pp. 100–2)) but with the emergence of such a group, 'war – and it is Surrealism's war – is declared on a world of surfaces' (Annette Michelson, quoted Lippard, 1970).

The radical aesthetic practices of Dada and Surrealism – dream work, collage, 'ready mades', etc. – are certainly relevant here. They are the classic modes of 'anarchic' discourse.[3] Breton's manifestos (1924 and 1929) established the basic premise of surrealism: that a new 'surreality' would emerge through the subversion of common sense, the collapse of prevalent logical categories and oppositions (e.g. dream/reality, work/play) and the celebration of the abnormal and the forbidden. This was to be achieved principally through a 'juxtaposition of two more or less distant realities' (Reverdy, 1918) exemplified for Breton in Lautréamont's bizarre phrase: 'Beautiful like the chance meeting of an umbrella and a sewing machine on a dissecting table' Lautréamont, 1970). In *The Crisis of the Object*, Breton further theorized this 'collage aesthetic', arguing rather optimistically that an assault on the syntax of everyday life which dictates the ways in which the most mundane objects are used, would instigate

. . . a *total revolution of the object*: acting to divert the object from its ends by coupling it to a new name and signing it. . . . Perturbation and deformation are in demand here for their own sakes. . . . Objects thus reassembled have in common the fact that they derive from and yet succeed in differing from the objects which surround us, by simple *change of role*. (Breton, 1936)

Max Ernst (1948) puts the same point more cryptically: 'He who says collage says the irrational'.

Obviously, these practices have their corollary in *bricolage*. The subcultural *bricoleur*, like the 'author' of a surrealist collage, typically 'juxtaposes two apparently incompatible realities (i.e. "flag": "jacket"; "hole": "teeshirt"; "comb: weapon") on an apparently unsuitable scale ... and ... it is there that the explosive junction occurs' (Ernst, 1948). Punk exemplifies most clearly the subcultural uses of these anarchic modes. It too attempted through 'perturbation and deformation' to disrupt and reorganize meaning. It, too, sought the 'explosive junction'. But what, if anything, were these subversive practices being used to signify? How do we 'read' them? By singling out punk for special attention, we can look more closely at some of the problems raised in a reading of style.

Style in revolt: Revolting style

Nothing was holy to us. Our movement was neither mystical, communistic nor anarchistic. All of these movements had some sort of programme, but ours was completely nihilistic. We spat on everything, including ourselves. Our symbol was nothingness, a vacuum, a void. (George Grosz on Dada)

We're so pretty, oh so pretty ... vac-unt. (The Sex Pistols)

Although it was often directly offensive (T-shirts covered in swear words) and threatening (terrorist/guerilla outfits) punk style was defined principally through the violence of its 'cut ups'. Like Duchamp's 'ready mades' – manufactured objects which qualified as art because he chose to call them such, the most unremarkable and inappropriate items – a pin, a plastic clothes peg, a television component, a razor blade, a tampon – could be brought within the province of punk (un)fashion. Anything within or without reason could be turned into part of what Vivien Westwood called 'confrontation dressing' so long as the rupture between 'natural' and constructed context was clearly visible (i.e. the rule would seem to be: if the cap doesn't fit, wear it).

Objects borrowed from the most sordid of contexts found a place in the punks' ensembles: lavatory chains were draped in graceful arcs across chests encased in plastic bin-liners. Safety pins were taken out of their domestic 'utility' context and worn as gruesome ornaments through the cheek, ear or lip. 'Cheap' trashy fabrics (PVC, plastic, lurex, etc.) in vulgar designs (e.g. mock leopard skin) and 'nasty' colours, long discarded by the quality end of the fashion industry as obsolete kitsch, were salvaged by the punks and turned into garments (fly boy drainpipes, 'common' miniskirts) which offered self-conscious commentaries on the notions of modernity and taste. Conventional ideas of prettiness were jettisoned along with the traditional feminine lore of cosmetics. Contrary to the advice of every woman's magazine, make-up for both boys and girls was worn to be seen. Faces became abstract portraits: sharply observed and meticulously executed studies in alienation. Hair was obviously dyed (hay yellow, jet black, or bright orange with tufts of green or bleached in question marks), and T-shirts and trousers told the story of their own construction with multiple zips and outside seams clearly displayed. Similarly, fragments of school uniform (white bri-nylon shirts, school ties) were symbolically defiled (the shirts covered in graffiti, or fake blood; the ties left undone) and juxtaposed against leather drains or shocking pink mohair tops. The perverse and the abnormal were valued intrinsically. In particular, the illicit iconography of sexual fetishism was used to predictable effect. Rapist masks and rubber wear, leather bodices and fishnet stockings, implausibly pointed stiletto heeled shoes, the whole paraphernalia of bondage – the belts, straps and chains – were exhumed from the boudoir, closet and the pornographic film and placed on the street where they retained their forbidden connotations. Some young punks even donned the dirty raincoat – that most prosaic symbol of sexual 'kinkiness' – and hence expressed their deviance in suitably proletarian terms.

Of course, punk did more than upset the wardrobe. It undermined every relevant discourse. Thus dancing, usually an involving and expressive medium in British rock and mainstream pop cultures, was turned into a dumbshow of blank robotics. Punk dances bore absolutely no relation to the desultory frugs and clinches which Geoff Mungham describes as intrinsic to the respectable working-class ritual of Saturday night at the Top Rank or Mecca.[4] Indeed, overt displays of heterosexual interest were generally regarded with contempt and suspicion (who let the BOF/ wimp[5] in?) and conventional courtship patterns found no place on the floor in dances like the pogo, the pose and the robot. Though the pose did allow for a minimum sociability (i.e. it could involve two people) the 'couple' were generally of the same sex and physical contact was ruled out of court as the relationship depicted in the dance was a 'professional' one. One participant would strike a suitable cliché fashion pose while the other would fall into a classic 'Bailey' crouch to snap an imaginary picture. The pogo forebade even this much interaction, though admittedly there was always a good deal of masculine jostling in front of the stage. In fact the pogo was a caricature – a *reductio ad absurdum* of all the solo dance styles associated with rock music. It resembled the 'anti-dancing' of the 'Leapniks' which Melly describes in connection with the trad boom (Melly, 1972). The same abbreviated gestures – leaping into the air, hands clenched to the sides, to head an imaginary ball – were repeated without variation in time to the strict mechanical rhythms of the music. In contrast to the hippies' languid, free-form dancing, and the 'idiot dancing' of the heavy metal rockers (see p. 155, n. 12), the pogo made improvisation redundant: the only variations were imposed by changes in the tempo of the music – fast numbers being 'interpreted' with manic abandon in the form of frantic on-the-spots, while the slower ones were pogoed with a detachment bordering on the catatonic.

The robot, a refinement witnessed only at the most exclusive punk gatherings, was both more 'expressive' and less spontaneous' within the very narrow range such terms acquired in punk usage. It consisted of barely perceptible twitches of the head and hands or more extravagant lurches (Frankenstein's first steps?) which were abruptly halted at random points. The resulting pose was held for several moments, even minutes, and the whole sequence was as suddenly, as unaccountably, resumed and re-enacted. Some zealous punks carried things one step further and choreographed whole evenings, turning themselves for a matter of hours, like Gilbert and George,[6] into automata, living sculptures.

The music was similarly distinguished from mainstream rock and pop. It was uniformly basic and direct in its appeal, whether through intention or lack of expertise. If the latter, then the punks certainly made a virtue of necessity ('We want to be amateurs' – Johnny Rotten). Typically, a barrage of guitars with the volume and treble turned to maximum accompanied by the occasional saxophone would pursue relentless (un)melodic lines against a turbulent background of cacophonous drumming and screamed vocals. Johnny Rotten succinctly defined punk's position on harmonics: 'We're into chaos not music'.

The names of the groups (the Unwanted, the Rejects, the Sex Pistols, the Clash, the Worst, etc.) and the titles of the songs: 'Belsen was a Gas', 'If You Don't Want to Fuck Me, fuck off', 'I Wanna be Sick on You', reflected the tendency towards wilful desecration and the voluntary assumption of outcast status which characterized the whole punk movement. Such tactics were, to adapt Levi-Strauss's famous phrase, 'things to whiten mother's hair with'. In the early days at least, these 'garage bands' could dispense with musical pretensions and substitute, in the traditional romantic terminology, 'passion' for 'technique', the language of the common man for the arcane posturings of the existing élite, the now familiar armoury of frontal attacks for the bourgeois notion of entertainment or the classical concept of 'high art'.

It was in the performance arena that punk groups posed the clearest threat to law and order. Certainly, they succeeded in subverting the conventions of concert and nightclub entertainment. Most significantly, they attempted both physically and in terms of lyrics and life-style to move closer to their audiences. This in itself is by no means unique: the boundary between artist and audience has often stood as a metaphor in revolutionary aesthetics (Brecht, the surrealists, Dada, Marcuse, etc.) for that larger and more intransigent barrier which separates art and the dream from reality and life under capitalism.[7] The stages of those venues secure enough to host 'new wave' acts were regularly invaded by hordes of punks, and if the management refused to tolerate such blatant disregard for ballroom etiquette, then the groups and their followers could be drawn closer together in a communion of spittle and mutual abuse. At the Rainbow Theatre in May 1977 as the Clash played 'White Riot', chairs were ripped out and thrown at the stage. Meanwhile, every performance, however apocalyptic, offered palpable evidence that things could change, indeed were changing: that performance itself was a possibility no authentic punk should discount. Examples abounded in the music press of 'ordinary fans' (Siouxsie of Siouxsie and the Banshees, Sid

Vicious of the Sex Pistols, Mark P of *Sniffin Glue*, Jordan of the Ants) who had made the symbolic crossing from the dance floor to the stage. Even the humbler positions in the rock hierarchy could provide an attractive alternative to the drudgery of manual labour, office work or a youth on the dole. The Finchley Boys, for instance, were reputedly taken off the football terraces by the Stranglers and employed as roadies.

If these 'success stories' were, as we have seen, subject to a certain amount of 'skewed' interpretation in the press, then there were innovations in other areas which made opposition to dominant definitions possible. Most notably, there was an attempt, the first by a predominantly working-class youth culture, to provide an alternative critical space within the subculture itself to counteract the hostile or at least ideologically inflected coverage which punk was receiving in the media. The existence of an alternative punk press demonstrated that it was not only clothes or music that could be immediately and cheaply produced from the limited resources at hand. The fanzines (*Sniffin Glue, Ripped and Torn,* etc.) were journals edited by an individual or a group, consisting of reviews, editorials and interviews with prominent punks, produced on a small scale as cheaply as possible, stapled together and distributed through a small number of sympathetic retail outlets.

The language in which the various manifestoes were framed was determinedly 'working class' (i.e. it was liberally peppered with swear words) and typing errors and grammatical mistakes, misspellings and jumbled pagination were left uncorrected in the final proof. Those corrections and crossings out that were made before publication were left to be deciphered by the reader. The overwhelming impression was one of urgency and immediacy, of a paper produced in indecent haste, of memos from the front line.

This inevitably made for a strident buttonholing type of prose which, like the music it described, was difficult to 'take in' in any quantity. Occasionally a wittier, more abstract item – what Harvey Garfinkel (the American ethnomethodologist) might call an 'aid to sluggish imaginations' – might creep in. For instance, *Sniffin Glue*, the first fanzine and the one which achieved the highest circulation, contained perhaps the single most inspired item of propaganda produced by the subculture – the definitive statement of punk's do-it-yourself philosophy – a diagram showing three finger positions on the neck of a guitar over the caption: 'Here's one chord, here's two more, now form your own band'.

Even the graphics and typography used on record covers and fanzines were homologous with punk's subterranean and anarchic style. The two typographic models were graffiti which was translated into a flowing 'spray can' script, and the ransom note in which individual letters cut up from a variety of sources (newspapers, etc.) in different type faces were pasted together to form an anonymous message. The Sex Pistols' 'God Save the Queen' sleeve (later turned into T-shirts, posters, etc.) for instance incorporated both styles: the roughly assembled legend was pasted across the Queen's eyes and mouth which were further disfigured by those black bars used in pulp detective magazines to conceal identity (i.e. they connote crime or scandal). Finally, the process of ironic self-abasement which characterized the subculture was extended to the name 'punk' itself which, with its derisory connotations of 'mean and petty villainy', 'rotten', 'worthless', etc. was generally preferred by hardcore members of the subculture to the more neutral 'new wave'.[8]

Hall *et al.* crossed the concepts of homology and *bricolage* to provide a systematic explanation of why a particular sub-cultural style should appeal to a particular group of people. The authors asked the question: 'What specifically does a subcultural style signify to the members of the subculture themselves?'

The answer was that the appropriated objects reassembled in the distinctive subcultural ensembles were 'made to reflect, express and resonate . . . aspects of group life' (Hall *et al.*, 1976b). The objects chosen were, either intrinsically or in their adapted forms, homologous with the focal concerns, activities, group structure and collective self-image of the subculture. They were 'objects in which (the subcultural members) could see their central values held and reflected' (Hall *et al.*, 1976b).

The skinheads were cited to exemplify this principle. The boots, braces and cropped hair were only considered appropriate and hence meaningful because they communicated the desired qualities: 'hardness, masculinity and working-classness'. In this way 'The symbolic objects – dress, appearance, language, ritual occasions, styles of interaction, music – were made to form a *unity* with the group's relations, situation, experience' (Hall *et al.*, 1976b).

The punks would certainly seem to bear out this thesis. The subculture was nothing if not consistent. There was a homological relation between the trashy cut-up clothes and spiky hair, the pogo and amphetamines, the spitting, the vomiting, the format of the fanzines, the insurrectionary poses and the 'soulless', frantically driven music. The punks wore clothes which were the sartorial equivalent of swear words, and they swore as they dressed – with calculated effect, lacing obscenities into record notes and publicity releases, interviews and love songs. Clothed in chaos, they produced Noise in the calmly orchestrated Crisis of everyday life in the late 1970s – a noise which made (no)sense in exactly the same way and to exactly the same extent as a piece of *avant-garde* music. If we were to write an epitaph for the punk subculture, we could do no better than repeat Poly Styrene's famous dictum: 'Oh Bondage, Up Yours!', or somewhat more concisely: the forbidden is permitted, but by the same token, nothing, not even these forbidden signifiers (bondage, safety pins, chains, hair-dye, etc.) is sacred and fixed.

This absence of permanently sacred signifiers (icons) creates problems for the semiotician. How can we discern any positive values reflected in objects which were chosen only to be discarded? For instance, we can say that the early punk ensembles gestured towards the signified's 'modernity' and 'working-classness'. The safety pins and bin liners signified a relative material poverty which was either directly experienced and exaggerated or sympathetically assumed, and which in turn was made to stand for the spiritual paucity of everyday life. In other words, the safety pins, etc. 'enacted' that transition from real to symbolic scarcity which Paul Piccone (1969) has described as the movement from 'empty stomachs' to 'empty spirits – and therefore an empty life notwithstanding [the] chrome and the plastic . . . of the life style of bourgeois society'.

We could go further and say that even if the poverty was being parodied, the wit was undeniably barbed; that beneath the clownish make-up there lurked the unaccepted and disfigured face of capitalism; that beyond the horror circus antics a divided and unequal society was being eloquently condemned. However, if we were to go further still and describe punk music as the 'sound of the Westway', or the pogo as the 'high-rise leap', or to talk of bondage as reflecting the narrow options of working-class youth, we would be treading on less certain ground. Such readings are both too literal and too conjectural. They are extrapolations from the subculture's own prodigious rhetoric, and rhetoric is not self-explanatory: it may say what it means but it does not necessarily 'mean' what it 'says'. In other words, it is opaque: its categories are part of its publicity. To return once more to Mepham (1974), 'The true text is reconstructed not by a process of piecemeal decoding, but by the identification of the generative sets of ideological categories and its replacement by a different set.'

To reconstruct the true text of the punk subculture, to trace the source of its subversive practices, we must first isolate the 'generative set' responsible for the subculture's exotic displays. Certain semiotic facts are undeniable. The punk subculture, like every other youth culture, was constituted in a series of spectacular transformations of a whole range of commodities, values, common-sense attitudes, etc. It was through these adapted forms that certain sections of predominantly working-class youth were able to restate their opposition to dominant values and institutions. However, when we attempt to close in on specific items, we immediately encounter problems. What, for instance, was the swastika being used to signify?

We can see how the symbol was made available to the punks (via Bowie and Lou Reed's 'Berlin' phase). Moreover, it clearly reflected the punks' interest in a decadent and evil Germany – a Germany which had 'no future'. It evoked a period redolent with a powerful mythology. Conventionally, as far as the British were concerned, the swastika signified 'enemy'. None the less, in punk usage, the symbol lost its 'natural' meaning – fascism. The punks were not generally sympathetic to the parties of the extreme right. On the contrary, as I have argued (see pp. 66–7) the conflict with the resurrected teddy boys and the widespread support for the anti-fascist movement (e.g. the Rock against Racism campaign) seem to indicate that the punk subculture grew up partly as an antithetical response to the re-emergence of racism in the mid-70s. We must resort, then, to the most obvious of explanations – that the swastika was worn because it was guaranteed to shock. (A punk asked by *Time Out* (17–23 December 1977) why she wore a swastika, replied: 'Punks just like to be hated'.) This represented more than a simple inversion or inflection of the ordinary meanings attached to an object. The signifier (swastika) had been wilfully detached from the concept (Nazism) it conventionally signified, and although it had been re-positioned (as 'Berlin') within an alternative subcultural context, its primary value and appeal derived precisely from its lack of meaning: from its potential for deceit. It was exploited as an empty effect. We are forced to the conclusion that the central value 'held and reflected' in the swastika was the communicated absence of any such identifiable values. Ultimately, the symbol was as 'dumb' as the rage it provoked. The key to punk style remains elusive. Instead of arriving at the point where we can begin to make sense of the style, we have reached the very place where meaning itself evaporates.

Style as signifying practice

> We are surrounded by emptiness but it is an emptiness filled with signs. (Lefebvre, 1971)

It would seem that those approaches to subculture based upon a traditional semiotics (a semiotics which begins with some notion of the 'message' – of a combination of elements referring unanimously to a fixed number of signifieds) fail to provide us with a 'way in' to the difficult and contradictory text of punk style. Any attempt at extracting a final set of meanings from the seemingly endless, often apparently random, play of signifiers in evidence here seems doomed to failure.

And yet, over the years, a branch of semiotics has emerged which deals precisely with this problem. Here the simple notion of reading as the revelation of a fixed number of concealed meanings is discarded in favour of the idea of *polysemy* whereby each text is seen to generate a potentially infinite range of meanings. Attention is consequently directed towards that point – or more precisely, that level – in any given text where the principle of meaning itself seems most in doubt. Such an approach lays less stress on the primacy of structure and system in language ('langue'), and more upon the *position* of the speaking subject in discourse ('parole'). It is concerned with the *process* of meaning-construction rather than with the final product.

Much of this work, principally associated with the *Tel Quel* group in France, has grown out of an engagement with literary and filmic texts. It involves an attempt to go beyond conventional theories of art (as mimesis, as representation, as a transparent reflection of reality, etc.) and to introduce instead 'the notion of art as "work", as "practice", as a particular *transformation* of reality, a version of reality, an account of reality'.[1]

One of the effects of this redefinition of interests has been to draw critical attention to the relationship between the means of representation and the object represented, between what in traditional aesthetics have been called respectively the 'form' and 'content' of a work of art. According to this approach, there can no longer be any absolute distinction between these two terms and the primary recognition that the *ways* in which things are said – the narrative structures employed – impose quite rigid limitations on *what* can be said is of course crucial. In particular, the notion that a detachable content can be inserted into a more or less neutral form – the assumption which seems to underpin the aesthetic of realism – is deemed illusory because such an aesthetic 'denies its own status as articulation. . . . [in this case] the real is not articulated, *it is*' (MacCabe, 1974)[2]

Drawing on an alternative theory of aesthetics, rooted in modernism and the *avant-garde* and taking as its model Brecht's idea of an 'epic theatre',[3] the *Tel Quel* group sets out to counter the prevailing notion of a transparent relation between sign and referent, signification and reality, through the concept of *signifying practice*. This phrase reflects exactly the group's central concerns with the ideological implications of form, with the idea of a positive construction and deconstruction of meaning, and with what has come to be called the 'productivity' of language. This approach sees language as an active, transitive force which shapes and positions the 'subject' (as speaker, writer, reader) while always itself remaining 'in process' capable of infinite adaptation. This emphasis on signifying practice is accompanied by a polemical insistence that art represents the triumph of process over fixity, disruption over unity, 'collision' over 'linkage'[4] – the triumph, that is, of the signifier over the signified. It should be seen as part of the group's attempt to substitute the values of 'fissure' and contradiction for the preoccupation with 'wholeness' (i.e. the text 'conceived as a closed structure' (Lackner and Matias, 1972)) which is said to characterize classic literary criticism.

Although much of this work is still at a tentative stage, it does offer a radically different perspective on style in subculture – one which assigns a central place to the problems of reading which we have encountered in our analysis of punk. Julia Kristeva's work on signification seems particularly useful. In *La Revolution du Langage Poetique* she explores the subversive possibilities within language through a study of French symbolist poetry, and points to 'poetic language' as the 'place where the social code is destroyed and renewed' (Kristeva, 1975). She counts as 'radical' those signifying practices which negate and disturb syntax – 'the condition of coherence and rationality' (White, 1977) – and which therefore serve to erode the concept of 'actantial position' upon which the whole 'Symbolic Order,'*[5] is seen to rest.

---

* The 'symbolic order' to which I have referred throughout should not be confused with Kristeva's 'Symbolic Order' which is used in a sense derived specifically from Lacanian psychoanalysis. I use the term merely to designate the apparent unity of the dominant ideological discourses in play at any one time.

Two of Kristeva's interests seem to coincide with our own: the creation of subordinate groups through *positioning in language* (Kristeva is specifically interested in women), and the disruption of the process through which such positioning is habitually achieved. In addition, the general idea of signifying practice (which she defines as 'the setting in place and cutting through or traversing of a system of signs'[6]) can help us to rethink in a more subtle and complex way the relations not only between marginal and mainstream cultural formations but between the various subcultural styles themselves. For instance, we have seen how all subcultural style is based on a practice which has much in common with the 'radical' collage aesthetic of surrealism and we shall be seeing how different styles represent different signifying practices. Beyond this I shall be arguing that the signifying practices embodied in punk were 'radical' in Kristeva's sense: that they gestured towards a 'nowhere' and actively *sought* to remain silent, illegible.

We can now look more closely at the relationship between experience, expression and signification in subculture; at the whole question of style and our reading of style. To return to our example, we have seen how the punk style fitted together homologically precisely through its lack of fit (hole: tee-shirt :: spitting : applause :: bin-liner : garment :: anarchy : order) – by its refusal to cohere around a readily identifiable set of central values. It cohered, instead, *elliptically* through a chain of conspicuous absences. It was characterized by its unlocatedness – its blankness – and in this it can be contrasted with the skinhead style.

Whereas the skinheads theorized and fetishized their class position, in order to effect a 'magical' return to an imagined past, the punks dislocated themselves from the parent culture and were positioned instead on the outside: beyond the comprehension of the average (wo)man in the street in a science fiction future. They played up their Otherness, 'happening' on the world as aliens, inscrutables. Though punk rituals, accents and objects were deliberately used to signify working-classness, the exact origins of individual punks were disguised or symbolically disfigured by the make-up, masks and aliases which seem to have been used, like Breton's art, as ploys 'to escape the principle of identity'.[7]

This workingclassness therefore tended to retain, *even in practice, even in its concretized forms*, the dimensions of an idea. It was abstract, disembodied, decontextualized. Bereft of the necessary details – a name, a home, a history – it refused to make sense, to be grounded, 'read back' to its origins. It stood in violent contradiction to that other great punk signifier – sexual 'kinkiness'. The two forms of deviance – social and sexual – were juxtaposed to give an impression of multiple warping which was guaranteed to disconcert the most liberal of observers, to challenge the glib assertions of sociologists no matter how radical. In this way, although the punks referred continually to the realities of school, work, family and class, these references only made sense at one remove: they were passed through the fractured circuitry of punk style and re-presented as 'noise', disturbance, entropy.

In other words, although the punks self-consciously mirrored what Paul Piccone (1969) calls the 'pre-categorical realities' of bourgeois society – inequality, powerlessness, alienation – this was only possible because punk style had made a decisive break not only with the parent culture but with its own *location in experience*. This break was both inscribed and re-enacted in the signifying practices embodied in punk style. The punk ensembles, for instance, did not so much magically resolve experienced contradictions as *re-present* the experience of contradiction itself in the form of visual puns (bondage, the ripped tee-shirt, etc.). Thus while it is true that the symbolic objects in punk style (the safety pins, the pogo, the ECT hairstyles) were 'made to form a "*unity*" with the group's relations, situations, experience' (Hall *et al.*, 1976b), this unity was at once 'ruptural' and 'expressive', or more precisely it expressed itself through rupture.

This is not to say, of course, that all punks were equally aware of the disjunction between experience and signification upon which the whole style was ultimately based. The style no doubt made sense for the first wave of self-conscious innovators at a level which remained inaccessible to those who became punks after the subculture had surfaced and been publicized. Punk is not unique in this: the distinction between originals and hangers-on is always a significant one in subculture. Indeed, it is frequently verbalized (plastic punks or safety-pin people, burrhead rastas or rasta bandwagon, weekend hippies, etc. versus the 'authentic' people). For instance, the mods had an intricate system of classification whereby the 'faces' and 'stylists' who made up the original coterie were defined against the unimaginative majority – the pedestrian 'kids' and 'scooter boys' who were accused of trivializing and coarsening the precious mod style. What is more, different youths bring different degrees of commitment to a subculture. It can represent a major dimension in people's lives – an axis erected in the face of the family around which a secret and immaculate identity can be made to cohere – or it can be a slight distraction, a bit of light relief from the monotonous but none the less paramount realities of school, home and work. It can be used as a means of escape, of total detachment from the surrounding terrain, or as a way of fitting back in to it and settling down after a week-end or evening spent letting off steam. In most cases it is used, as Phil Cohen suggests, magically to achieve both ends. However, despite these individual differences, the members of a subculture must share a common language. And if a style is really to catch on, if it is to become genuinely popular, it must say the right things in the right way at the right time. It must anticipate or encapsulate a mood, a moment. It must embody a sensibility, and the sensibility which punk style embodied was essentially dislocated, ironic and self-aware.

Just as individual members of the same subculture can be more or less conscious of what they are saying in style and in what ways they are saying it, so different subcultural styles exhibit different degrees of rupture. The conspicuously scruffy, 'unwholesome' punks obtruded from the familiar landscape of normalized forms in a more startling fashion than the mods, tellingly described in a newspaper of the time as '. . . pin-neat, lively and clean', although the two groups had none the less engaged in the same signifying practice (i.e. self-consciously subversive *bricolage*).

This partly explains or at least underpins internal sub-cultural hostilities. For example, the antagonism between the teddy boy revivalists and the punk rockers went beyond any simple incompatability at the level of 'content' – different music, dress, etc. – beyond even the different political and racial affiliations of the two groups (see p. 67), the different relationships with the parent community, etc. (see pp. 81–4) and was inscribed in the very way in which the two styles were constructed: the way in which they communicated (or refused to communicate) meaning. Teddy boys interviewed in the press regularly objected to the punks' symbolic 'plundering' of the precious 50s ward-robe (the drains, the winklepickers, quiffs, etc.) and to the ironic and impious uses to which these 'sacred' artefacts were put when 'cut up' and reworked into punk style where presumably they were contaminated by association (placed next to 'bovver boots' and latex bondage-wear!).[8] Behind punk's favoured 'cut ups' lay hints of disorder, of breakdown and category confusion: a desire not only to erode racial and gender boundaries but also to confuse chronological sequence by mixing up details from different periods.

As such, punk style was perhaps interpreted by the teddy boys as an affront to the traditional working-class values of forthrightness, plain speech and sexual puritanism which they had endorsed and revived. Like the reaction of the rockers to the mods and the skinheads to the hippies, the teddy boy revival seems to have represented an 'authentic' working-class backlash to the proletarian posturings of the new wave. *The way in which it signified*, via a magical return to the past, to the narrow confines of the community and the parent culture, to the familiar and the legible, was perfectly in tune with its inherent conservatism.[9] Not only did the teds react aggressively to punk objects and 'meanings', they also reacted to the way in which those objects were presented, those meanings constructed and dismantled. They did so by resorting to an altogether more primitive 'language': by turning back, in George Melly's words (1972), to a ' "then" which was superior to "now" ' which, as Melly goes on to say, is 'a very anti-pop concept'.

We can express the difference between the two practices in the following formula: one (i.e. the punks') is kinetic, transitive and concentrates attention on *the act of transformation* performed upon the object: the other (i.e. the teds') is static, expressive, and concentrates attention on the *objects-in-themselves*. We can perhaps grasp the nature of this distinction more clearly if we resort to another of Kristeva's categories – '*signifiance*'. She has introduced this term to describe the work of the signifier in the text in contrast to signification which refers to the work of the signified. Roland Barthes defines the difference between the two operations thus:

> Signifiance is a *process* in the course of which the 'subject' of the text, escaping (conventional logic) and engaging in other logics (of the signifier, of contradiction) struggles with meaning and is deconstructed ('lost'); signifiance – and this is what immediately distinguishes it from signification – is thus precisely a work; not the work by which the (intact and exterior) subject might try to master the

language . . . but that radical work (leaving nothing intact) through which the subject explores – entering not
observing – how the language works and undoes him or
her. . . . Contrary to signification, signifiance cannot be
reduced therefore, to communication, representation, expression: it places the subject (of writer, reader) in the
text not as a projection . . . but as a 'loss', a 'disappearance'. (see Heath, 1977)

Elsewhere, in an attempt to specify the various kinds of
meaning present in film, Barthes refers to the 'moving play'
of signifiers as the 'third (obtuse) meaning' (the other two
meanings being the 'informational' and the 'symbolic'
which, as they are 'closed' and 'obvious' are normally the
only ones which concern the semiotician). The third meaning works against ('exceeds') the other two by 'blunting'
them – rounding off the 'obvious signified' and thus causing
'the reading to slip'. Barthes uses as an example a still from
Eisenstein's film *Battleship Potemkin* which shows an old
woman, a headscarf pulled low over her forehead, caught in
a classical, grief-stricken posture. At one level, the level of
the obvious meaning, she seems to typify 'noble grief' but, as
Barthes observes, her strange headdress, and rather 'stupid'
fish-like eyes cut across this typification in such a way that
'there is no guarantee of intentionality' (Barthes, 1977a).
This, the third meaning, flows upstream as it were, against
the supposed current of the text, preventing the text from
reaching its destination: a full and final closure. Barthes thus
describes the third meaning as 'a gash rased [sic] of meaning
(of the desire for meaning) . . . it outplays meaning – subverts not the content but the whole practice of meaning'.

The ideas of 'signifiance' and 'obtuse meaning' suggest
the presence in the text of an intrinsically subversive component. Our recognition of the operations performed within
the text at the level of the signifier can help us to understand
the way in which certain subcultural styles seem to work

against the reader and to resist any authorative interpretation. If we consider for a moment it becomes clear that not all subcultural styles 'play' with language to the same extent: some are more 'straightforward' than others and place a higher priority on the construction and projection of a firm and coherent identity. For instance, if we return to our earlier example, we could say that whereas the teddy boy style says its piece in a relatively direct and obvious way, and remains resolutely committed to a 'finished' meaning, to the signified, to what Kristeva calls 'signification', punk style is in a constant state of assemblage, of flux. It introduces a heterogeneous set of signifiers which are liable to be superseded at any moment by others no less productive. It invites the reader to 'slip into' 'signifiance' to lose the sense of direction, the direction of sense. Cut adrift from meaning, the punk style thus comes to approximate the state which Barthes has described as 'a *floating* (the very form of the signifier); a floating which would not destroy anything but would be content simply to disorientate the Law' (Barthes, 1977b).

The two styles, then, represent different signifying practices which confront the reader with quite different problems. We can gauge the extent of this difference (which is basically a difference in the degree of *closure*) by means of an analogy. In *The Thief's Journal*, Genet contrasts his relationship to the elusive Armand with his infatuation with the more transparent Stilittano in terms which underline the distinction between the two practices: 'I compare Armand to the expanding universe. . . . Instead of being defined and reduced to observable limits, Armand constantly changes as I pursue him. On the other hand, Stilittano is already encircled' (Genet, 1967).

The relationship between experience, expression and signification is therefore not a constant in subculture. It can form a unity which is either more or less organic, striving towards some ideal coherence, or more or less ruptural, reflecting the experience of breaks and contradictions. More-over, individual subcultures can be more or less 'conserva-tive' or 'progressive', integrated *into* the community, con-tinuous with the values of that community, or extrapolated *from* it, defining themselves *against* the parent culture. Finally, these differences are reflected not only in the objects of subcultural style, but in the signifying practices which re-present those objects and render them meaningful.

NINE

O.K., it's Culture, but is it Art?

Painting is jewellery . . . collage is poor. (Louis Aragon)

How, in the final analysis, are we to make sense of subcultural style? One of the more obvious ways is to 'appreciate' it in orthodox aesthetic terms. Much of the writing on pop culture, although conceived in a spirit of revenge for the cursory attention paid to it by more conservative writers, has tended at some stage to lose its rebellious edge and to resort instead to that most traditional of defences: that pop music and the associated graphics are 'at least as good as high art' (see, for instance, the closing chapter of Melly's otherwise excellent *Revolt into Style*). Occasionally, this reverential treatment was even extended to a feature of subcultural style:

> Very little has come out of the whole teenage development that has more beauty than decorated rocker jackets. They show the creative impulse at its purest and most inventive. Without any sentimentality, it is possible to say that they constitute art of a high degree, symmetrical, ritualistic, with a bizarre metallic brilliance and a high fetishistic power. (Nuttal, 1969)[1]

One cannot help but feel that this misses the point. Subcultures are not 'cultural' in this sense, and the styles with which they are identified cannot be adequately or usefully described as 'art of a high degree'. Rather they manifest culture in the broader sense, as systems of communication, forms of expression and representation. They conform to the structural anthropologists' definition of culture as 'coded exchanges of reciprocal messages'.[2] In the same way, subcultural styles do indeed qualify as art but as art in (and out of) particular contexts; not as timeless objects, judged by the immutable criteria of traditional aesthetics, but as 'appropriations', 'thefts', subversive transformations, as *movement*.

We have seen how these styles can be described as forms of signifying practice. But if Kristeva's thesis seems unnecessarily complex for our purposes (perhaps more to the point, if I have damaged its coherence by taking pieces out of context) then there is general agreement among those critics who work within a structuralist perspective that both artistic expression and aesthetic pleasure are intimately bound up with the destruction of existing codes and the formulation of new ones:

> . . . aesthetic expression aims to communicate notions, subtleties, complexities, which have not yet been formulated, and, therefore, as soon as an aesthetic order comes to be generally perceived as a code (as a way of expressing notions which have already been formulated), then works of art tend to move beyond this code while exploring its possible mutations and extensions. . . . Much of the interest of works of art lies in the ways in which they explore and modify the codes which they seem to be using. (Culler, 1976)

It is through a dialectic of the kind that Jonathan Culler describes here that subcultural styles are created, adapted and eventually superseded. Indeed, the succession of postwar youth styles can be represented on the formal level as a series of transformations of an initial set of items (clothes, dance, music, argot) unfolding through an internal set of polarities (mod v. rocker, skinhead v. greaser, skinhead v. hippie, punk v. hippie, ted v. punk, skinhead v. punk[3]) and defined against a parallel series of 'straight' transformations ('high'/mainstream fashion). Each subculture moves through a cycle of resistance and defusion and we have seen how this cycle is situated within the larger cultural and commercial matrices. Subcultural deviance is simultaneously rendered 'explicable' and meaningless in the classrooms, courts and media at the same time as the 'secret' objects of subcultural style are put on display in every high street record shop and chain-store boutique. Stripped of its unwholesome connotations, the style becomes fit for public consumption. André Masson has described (1945) how the same process contributed to the decline of surrealism:

> This meeting of an umbrella and a sewing machine on the operating table happened only once. Traced, repeated over and over again, mechanised, the unusual vulgarises itself. . . . A painful 'fantasy' can be seen in the street shop windows.

Cut ups and collages, no matter how bizarre, do not change so much as rearrange things, and needless to say, the 'explosive junction' never occurs: no amount of stylistic incantation can alter the oppressive mode in which the commodities used in subculture have been produced.

None the less style does have its moment, its brief outrageous spectacle, and in our study of style in subculture we should focus on that moment, on the fact of transformation rather than on the objects-in-themselves. Returning to our rocker jackets, we can agree with Nuttall that they do indeed constitute objects endowed with a 'high fetishistic power'. However, we should not attempt to lift them too far from the contexts in which they are produced and worn. If we are to think in formal terms at all, subcultural styles are more usefully regarded as mutations and extensions of existing codes rather than as the 'pure' expression of creative drives, and above all they should be seen as *meaningful* mutations. Sometimes these forms will be disfigured and disfiguring. At such times, no doubt, this will be their 'point'. They are counterposed against the symbolic order of structured appearances – the syntax which positions the producer over and against that which he or she produces. In the face of such an order, they are bound on occasion to assume monstrous and unnatural features.

Much of this book has been based on the assumption that the two positions 'Negro' and 'white working-class youth' can be equated. This equation is no doubt open to dispute; it cannot be tested by the standard sociological procedures. Though it is undeniably there in the social structure, it is there as an immanence, as a submerged possibility, as an existential option; and one cannot verify an existential option scientifically – you either see it or you don't.

However, other objections might be raised. To lay too much emphasis on the connection between the two groups does a disservice to a black community formed in centuries of the most naked oppression imaginable: a culture which, for better or worse, bears the stamp of a singular history and which, moreover, has at last begun to break away from the Master, to cohere in ethnicity. The relationships between young and old, child and parent are, as a result, differently structured in black and white communities. Reggae is not just for the young, and though adult West Indians no doubt prefer their rhythms lighter and less African, both young and old are part of the same defensively organized collective, tied together by the same lack of options, the same limited mobility.

Thus, while white working-class youths will in all probability remain working class throughout their lives, they will eventually grow up and settle down to a place if not in the sun then at least in the consensus. Blacks, on the other hand, never lose what is, in our society, the disability of blackness. They seem likely, at least for the foreseeable future, to remain at the bottom of the heap. None the less, one may assume that these differences will be gradually eroded as the black presence becomes more established (already there are signs in the black community of a growing generational consciousness amongst the 'youth') and as long as we do not collapse the two positions, a comparison between black and white subcultures can prove illuminating. For example, we have seen how they produce similar reactions from the press and the judiciary. Reggae is as likely as punk rock to be dismissed by 'serious' people as nonsense or as an irrelevant distraction from the major issues of life in contemporary Britain. Elsewhere, both forms are liable to be condemned as degenerate or reduced to 'good clean fun'. But there is also, as we have seen, a deeper correspondence between them: both reggae and punk rock are created within the contexts of subcultures which are themselves produced in response to specific historical conditions. This response embodies a Refusal: it begins with a movement away from the consensus (and in Western democracies, the consensus is sacred). It is the unwelcome revelation of difference which draws down upon the members of a subculture hostility, derision, 'white and dumb rages'.

Subcultures are therefore expressive forms but what they express is, in the last instance, a fundamental tension between those in power and those condemned to subordinate positions and second-class lives. This tension is figuratively expressed in the form of subcultural style and it is appropriate that we should turn here to a metaphor for our final definition of subculture. In one of his most influential essays 'Ideology and Ideological State Apparatuses', Althusser describes how the different parts of the social formation – the family, education, the mass media, cultural and political institutions – together serve to perpetuate submission to the ruling ideology. However, these institutions do not perform this function through the direct transmission of 'ruling ideas'. Instead, it is the way in which they work together in what Althusser calls a 'teeth-gritting harmony' that the ruling ideology is reproduced 'precisely in its contradictions'. Throughout this book, I have interpreted subculture as a form of resistance in which experienced contradictions and objections to this ruling ideology are obliquely represented in style. Specifically I have used the term 'noise' to describe the challenge to symbolic order that such styles are seen to constitute. Perhaps it would be more accurate and more telling to think of this noise as the flip-side to Althusser's 'teeth-gritting harmony' (Althusser, 1971b).

CONCLUSION

At best, daily life, like art, is revolutionary. At worst it is a prison-house. (Paul Willis, 1977)

Prison serves no purpose. . . . The time for blues is over. (Genet, 1971)

THIS book opened with the writer Jean Genet paying homage to his phantom lovers – a collection of mug-shots stuck with ingenious skill to the back of a sheet of prison regulations. We end with the same author outside the walls of a different prison looking up to another, younger inmate – George Jackson. His love for the young criminal, though no less tender, is tempered with compassion. It has become a fuller, deeper bond through Genet's decision to recognize an Other and share in his suffering. Genet has won sainthood at last but only by transcending the terms in which it was originally conceived – by substituting brother-hood for selfhood. Times have changed. Genet has moved through art from the practice of crime to an idea of crime and from there towards a theory of revolution. He has moved from individual to general causes. He is now a famous writer. Genet is no typical ex-con and George Jack-son was no ordinary criminal. He too was about to be acknowledged as a writer. Sentenced at the age of eighteen to 'one year to life,[1] for robbing a petrol station of 70 dollars, Jackson was one of the first of a new breed of long-term prisoners who took advantage of the ample time and solitude to educate themselves, to theorize their positions and gain a political perspective on their criminal careers. In 1970, along with two other inmates from Soledad prison, he was facing trial and a possible death sentence for the murder of a prison guard. The trial had assumed a wider political significance because the three stood together, were militant and articulate. What is more, they were black. Times indeed have changed.

Genet's Introduction to *Soledad Brother: The Prison Letters of George Jackson* has one principal theme: that black writers striving to express themselves in the language of the Master are caught in a double bind: 'It is perhaps a new source of anguish for the black man to realise that if he writes a masterpiece, it is his enemy's language, his enemy's treasury which is enriched by the additional jewel he has so furiously and lovingly carved' (Genet, 1971). Genet recognizes in the work of the new black writers two ways out of this conundrum. First, the religion of the Enemy can be used against the Enemy. Stripped of the 'presbyterian and Biblical rags', they can learn to denounce in voices 'blacker and more angry . . . the curse not of being black but captive'. Second, as these new writers are condemned to speak forever in an alien tongue which draws them closer to the Enemy, they must seek to root out the Master in language. An exile like Jackson, a victim, in his own words, of the 'new slavery', has only one recourse: 'to accept this language but to corrupt it so skilfully that the white men are caught in his trap', and once caught, they can be symbolically annihilated.

Genet warns us that the letters do not make easy reading. There can be no easy access for us. Rather they have been written between clenched teeth in hard, ugly words, '. . . the forbidden words, the accursed words, the words covered with blood, the dangerous words, the padlocked words, the words that do not belong to the dictionary . . .' (Genet, 1971). So Genet brings us full circle. He brings us back to an image of graffiti, to a group of blacks, immured in language, kicking against the white-washed walls of two types of prison – the real and the symbolic. By this indirect route, he brings us back also to the meaning of style in subculture and to the messages which lie behind disfigurement. To stretch the metaphor a little further, we could say that the sub-cultural styles which we have been studying, like prison graffiti, merely pay tribute to the place in which they were produced, and '. . . it is prudent . . . that any text which reaches us from this . . . place should reach us as though mutilated' (Genet, 1971).

In the course of this book, we have learned like Genet to be suspicious of the common-sense categories which are brought to bear on subculture. We have had to expand our definition of culture to cover all those expressive forms which give meaningful shape to group experience. To arrive at this definition, we have moved through a tradition which en-compasses talents as diverse as those of T. S. Eliot, Roland Barthes and Jean Genet. In a sense, these three writers have presided over our study throughout, providing the basic frames of reference. They have all supplied us with lists of the most unremarkable phenomena which none the less hold for each writer a particular significance. First, Eliot gives us our primary definition of culture. He finds 'in all the characteristic activities and interests of a people' – in Derby Day, beetroot and the dogs – a meaningful coherence, a 'whole way of life'. Together these elements add up to an order, an Englishness which he feels is worth endorsing; a tradition which he is pledged to defend against the vulgar inroads of mass culture: the trashy films, the comics, the mean emotions and petty lives of all the faithless 'hollow men'.

Barthes' list, compiled in a spirit no less detached, illustrates a somewhat different perspective. He too adopts a prophetic tone, but where Eliot is Anglo-Catholic and conservative, Barthes is materialist and Marxist. Eliot's dark night of the soul ('Men and bits of paper whirling in the cold wind/That blows before and after time' (Eliot, 1959) has been replaced by Barthes' 'dark night of history' where 'the future becomes an essence, the essential destruction of the past' (Barthes, 1972). Both are alienated from the forms of contemporary culture, but where Eliot finds sanctuary in the British heritage, in prayer and holy wafers, Barthes 'cannot see the Promised Land. For him, tomorrow's positivity is entirely hidden by today's negativity' (Barthes, 1972). Barthes is not concerned to make distinctions between high and low culture: everything from our theatre, and a murder trial, to the cooking we dream of is cursed, enmeshed for Barthes in a pernicious ideology. Everything nourishing is spoiled; every spontaneous event or emotion a potential prey to myth. Barthes can offer no salvation but at least there is a purgatory in reading: myths are signs, and signs if nothing else are legible. Barthes, then, supplied us with a method – a way of reading style.

We come at last to Genet, who furnished a metaphor and a model, for, despite the initial misfortunes of his birth and position, he has learned to live 'in style'. Genet is a subculture unto himself. His tastes are as refined as Barthes'. He has Barthes' eye for detail, his sense of words. His style is equally precious. Like Barthes also, he has secret insights, he is involved in undercover work. But he is differently placed. He is a thief, a liar, a 'jerk'.[2] Unlike Barthes he has been excluded by order of the State. He is 'in solitary'. Admittedly, he begins a Catholic but this does not save him, for unlike Eliot he is illegitimate. His Catholicism is strictly of the peasant variety. It stops at the icons and the altar rail. It is pagan and idolatrous. Moreover, he finds in the negation of his faith an underneath – a 'seamy side' – which is more to his liking. He becomes, like his fictional Maids, the 'unwholesome exhalation' of his Master.[3] He turns a system on its head. He 'chooses' his crimes, his sexuality, the repugnance and outrage he arouses in the streets, and when he looks at the world, 'nothing is irrelevant': the stock-market quotations, the style of the judiciary, the flower beds have a meaning – his Otherness, his Exile. Genet is as finicky as Eliot about where he dispenses his favours: only the worst is good enough for him, nowhere but the lowest and most sordid dive can be called home. Positioned on the outside (even when 'inside') Genet not only reads the signs, he writes them. He subverts appearances, slips behind them to have a joke at their expense: on July 14, the day of the tricoleur, he 'dresses up in all the other colours out of consideration for them because they are disdained' (Genet, 1966a). Finally, he turns to language, but he comes to it via a secret route. He enters it by a back passage violently to 'possess' a language which he can no more call his own than can the blacks. Once there, he disrupts it, pushes its words into forbidden places. He makes it over into his own 'unnatural' image.[4]

Of the three writers, Genet is closest to the object of our study. His life and work have been used throughout as a model for the construction of style in subculture. The emphasis has thus been placed on deformity, transformation and Refusal. As a result, this book no doubt succumbs to a kind of romanticism. Certainly we have strayed far from those areas which are deemed the legitimate concern of sociologists, even radical ones. I have not attempted to provide a systematic explanation of the 'problem' of deviance, nor to look in detail at the various agencies of social control (the police, school, etc.) which play a crucial role in determining subculture. On the other hand, I have tried to avoid the temptation to portray subculture (as some writers influenced by Marcuse were once prone to do)[5] as the repository of 'Truth', to locate in its forms some obscure revolutionary potential. Rather I have sought, in Sartre's words, to acknowledge the right of the subordinate class (the young, the black, the working class) to 'make something of what is made of (them)'[6] – to embellish, decorate, parody and wherever possible to recognize and rise above a subordinate position which was never of their choosing.

However, we should be foolish to think that by tackling a subject so manifestly popular as youth style, we have resolved any of the contradictions which underlie contemporary cultural studies. Such a resolution would be, as Cohen puts it, purely 'magical'. It is highly unlikely, for instance, that the members of any of the subcultures described in this book would recognize themselves reflected here. They are still less likely to welcome any efforts on our part to understand them.[7] After all, we, the sociologists and interested straights, threaten to kill with kindness the forms which we seek to elucidate. When the first impulse of Fanon's black man 'is to say no to all those who attempt to build a definition of him' (Fanon, 1967) we should hardly be surprised to find our 'sympathetic' readings of subordinate culture are regarded by the members of a subculture with just as much indifference and contempt as the hostile labels imposed by the courts and the press. In this respect to get the point is, in a way, to miss the point.

Thus, while Genet embodies our object most clearly, in the end Barthes is closest to us. He understands the problems of the reader – the 'mythologist' who can no longer be one with the 'myth-consumers'.[8] For, like Barthes, we must live an uneasy cerebral relation to the bric-à-brac of life – the mundane forms and rituals whose function it is to make us feel at home, to reassure us, to fill up the gap between desire and fulfilment. Instead, they summon up for us the very fears which they alleviate for others. Their arbitrary nature stands revealed: the apparent can no longer be taken for granted. The cord has been cut: we are cast in a marginal role. We are in society but not inside it, producing analyses of popular culture which are themselves anything but popular. We are condemned to a 'theoretical sociality' (Barthes, 1972) 'in camera' to the text – caught between the object and our reading:

> . . . we constantly drift between the object and its de-mystification, powerless to render its wholeness. For if we penetrate the object, we liberate it but destroy it; and if we acknowledge its full weight, we respect it, but re-store it to a state which is still mystified. (Barthes, 1972)

The study of subcultural style which seemed at the outset to draw us back towards the real world, to reunite us with 'the people', ends by merely confirming the distance between the reader and the 'text', between everyday life and the 'mythologist' whom it surrounds, fascinates and finally excludes. It would seem that we are still, like Barthes (1972), 'condemned for some time yet to speak *excessively* about reality'.

REFERENCES

Chapter 1

1 Although Williams had posited a new, broader definition of culture, he intended this to complement rather than contradict earlier formulations:

> It seems to me that there is value in each of these kinds of definition. . . . the degree to which we depend, in our knowledge of many past societies and past stages of our own, on the body of intellectual and imaginative work which has retained its major communicative power, makes the description of culture in these terms if not complete, then at least reasonable . . . there are elements in the 'ideal' definition which . . . seem to me valuable. (Williams, 1965)

2 In his *Course in General Linguistics*, Saussure stressed the arbitrary nature of the linguistic sign. For Saussure, language is a system of mutually related values, in which arbitrary 'signifiers' (e.g. words) are linked to equally arbitrary 'signifieds' ('concepts . . . negatively defined by their relations with other terms in the system') to form signs. These signs together constitute a system. Each element is defined through its position within the rele-

vant system – its relation to other elements – through the dialectics of identity and difference. Saussure postulated that other systems of significance (e.g. fashion, cookery) might be studied in a similar way, and that eventually linguistics would form part of a more general science of signs – a semiology.

3 The fashionable status of this word has in recent years contributed to its indiscriminate use. I intend here the very precise meaning established by Louis Althusser: 'the *problematic* of a word or concept consists of the theoretical or ideological framework within which that word or concept can be used to establish, determine and discuss a particular range of issues and a particular kind of problem' (Althusser and Balibar, 1968; see also Bennett, 1979).

Chapter 2

1 Although groups like London SS had prepared the way for punk throughout 1975, it wasn't until the appearance of the Sex Pistols that punk began to emerge as a recognizable style. The first review of the group which, for the press at least, always embodied the essence of punk, appeared in the *New Musical Express*, 21 February 1976. The most carefully documented moment of this early period was the Sex Pistols' performance at the Nashville in West Kensington in April, during which Johnny Rotten allegedly left the stage in order to help a supporter involved in a fight. However, it wasn't until the summer of 1976 that punk rock began to attract critical attention, and we can date the beginning of the moral panic to September 1976 when a girl was partially blinded by a flying beer glass during the two-day punk festival at the 100 Club in Soho.

Chapter 3

1 See Dilip Hiro's *Black British, White British* for a brief but perceptive account of the development of Jamaican patois. Despite the fact that communication was generally discouraged by the slave owners (e.g. slaves from different tribes were mixed together) the slaves learned to speak a modified version of seventeenth-century colloquial English by surreptitious means (e.g. by lip-reading and imitation).

2 Rocksteady was an intermediate phase in the development of Jamaican popular music, sandwiched between ska and reggae. Though slower and stickier than the jumpy, somewhat raucous ska, rocksteady was replaced by the even tighter, heavier, more 'African' reggae in the late 60s.

3 This is actually recreated in the sound system sessions in which the d-j 'talks over' the studio product and becomes what I-Roy, himself a talk-over artist, calls 'the medium through which the people speak' (B.B.C. radio interview broadcast, July 1977).

4 North American black ghetto culture is similarly saturated in Biblical language. For a redefinition of Christian terminology which parallels the appropriations of the Rastafari movement, one need only mention the U.S. concept 'soul' which describes a musical genre (black r & b) and a whole set of black attitudes, scrupulously bracketed off by the more militant young blacks from the 'blues' and the accompanying 'Uncle Tom' attitudes (see Hannerz, 1969; Le-Roi Jones, 1975).

5 Dreadlocks, the long, plaited hair worn by some Rastafarians, were originally intended to reproduce the 'ethnic' look of some East African tribes. Subsequently, Biblical exhortations to leave the 'locks unshorn', and the cautionary tale of Samson and Delilah were also used to justify the Rasta's unconventional appearance. The

locks became one of the most sensational aspects of the Rasta 'style' (along with ganja, i.e. marijhuana), focusing attention on the movement and attracting widespread censure. The locks became the most readily identifiable signifier of a meaningful difference. Reggae lyrics by 'Rasta' artists show particular concern for dreadlocks: e.g. 'Don't touch I-Man Locks' – I-Roy (Virgin, 1976).

6 Jamaica was granted independence in 1962. The new government took as its motto: 'Out of many, one people'.

7 Michael Manley has headed the P.N.P. administration since 1972 (re-elected 1976). He has been responsible for injecting a specifically Caribbean blend of populism and Biblical rhetoric into Jamaican politics. He incorporates reggae and religious metaphors into his election campaigns, and his most recent slogan 'Under Heavy Manners' (which refers to the 1976 State of Emergency) has been assimilated into the vocabulary of reggae as a particularly potent and expressive formula.

8 This shift is neatly summed up in the replacement of tourism by reggae as the country's second largest industry (next to bauxite mining). The setting up of sugar co-operatives, the Cuban financing of schools and the ecstatic reception given the Cuban contingent at the 1976 Cari-festa, even the re-election of Manley in the same year, all indicate a movement away from the older Euro-American influences.

9 The dub is the instrumental ridim-track – an unobstructed rhythm without words with the emphasis on the bass. Sound effects and echo in particular are used a lot. It is, in the words of Dermott Hussey, 'a naked dance rhythm', and the producer and the engineer have become the acknowledged 'artists' of the dub. Across the dub, the 'talk-over' artist improvises a spoken 'toast' which is generally organized around 'black' themes.

10 'Rockers' – 'heavy' or 'ethnic' reggae. The term first appeared in early summer 1976.

11 The rude boys formed a deviant subculture in Jamaica in the mid to late 60s. Flashy, urban 'rough and tough', they were glamorized in a string of reggae and rocksteady hits: 'Rudy a Message To You' – Dandy Livingstone; 'Rude Boy' – the Wailers; 'Shanty Town' – Desmond Dekker; 'Johnny Too Bad' – the Slickers.

12 The 'toast' is a monologue delivered live by a 'talk-over' d-j as an instrumental dub is being played over the sound system. See n. 9.

13 'Dread' is a polysemantic term. It seems to encompass righteousness, Biblical 'wrath' and the fear inspired by that wrath.

14 The violence at the 1976 Carnival was triggered off by the conspicuous presence of large numbers of policemen in the Acklam Road area where several sound-systems were positioned under the fly-over. The less serious disturbances of the 1977 Carnival also centred on this officially recognized 'trouble-spot'. When Sir Robert Mark assured the public in the wake of the 1976 riots that he would not tolerate a 'no-go area', one suspects he was referring specifically to the sound-systems in the Acklam Road.

15 A police raid on the Carib Club in the autumn of 1974 triggered off a pitched battle which resulted in the arrest and subsequent acquittal of four black youths.

16 See Tolson (1977), who is concerned with how ideological constructs about 'keeping your place', etc. are manifested in the patterns of working-class speech.

17 Ulf Hannerz has noted a similar transformation in American ghetto-culture, and associated these changing patterns of physical movement with an adjustment in the self-concept of younger blacks. He suggests that the younger blacks are defining themselves against the down-home parent culture and quotes one respondent

who explicitly identifies the shuffle with an outmoded deference and submissiveness: 'They [the "Uncle Toms"] say "Yes sir", "No sir". They gonna shuffle forever' (Hannerz, 1969).

18 The mid-60s saw a growing consciousness of colour among urban American blacks which was reflected in the work of artists like James ('Say it Loud, I'm Black and I'm Proud') Brown and Bobby Bland. Charlie Gillet documents this period comprehensively in *Sound of the City*.

19 'Humble Lion' and 'steppers' replaced 'rockers' as the in-term for 'heavy reggae' and dub, in May 1977 (see *Black Echoes*, 18 July 1977).

20 The Rasta preoccupation with 'nature' and 'natural man' is reflected in the lyrics of the songs. Big Youth dismisses Babylon materials in a celebrated mock-serious talk-over 'Natty no Jester' (Klik, 1975):

'Cos natty dread no jester
He no wear no polyester. . . .

21 In *The Jazz Life* Nat Hentoff describes how a mythical association between heroin addiction and inspiration in jazz developed in the 1950s. Young musicians, attempting to reproduce the 'hard' sound of Charlie Parker and Fats Navarro (both heroin addicts) were drawn towards what Hentoff calls 'emulation-by-needle'. Le-Roi Jones, in *Blues People*, defines heroin usage as a 'kind of one-upmanship of the highest order' which turns the 'Negro's separation from the mainstream of . . . society into an advantage'. White hipsters, intent on translating their emotional affinities with blacks into actual terms found heroin appealing at the same symbolic level (see also Harold Finestone, 'Cats, Kicks and Colour' in *The Other Side*).

Chapter 4

1 Of course these charges cannot be levelled against the authentic black 'swing' bands (Count Basie, Duke Ellington, etc.).

2 Charlie Parker (1920–1955) was the most celebrated exponent of be-bop. The be-bop style, developed during the late 1940s and early 1950s, consisted of long, elaborate improvizations around a standard chord sequence. These improvizations were experimental and often apparently 'discordant', and the rupture with the white classical music tradition was quite deliberate (e.g. the distinctive polyrhythmic drumming was called 'dropping bombs' in jazz argot). According to Hentoff, the expression 'playing white' or 'ofay' was one of the strongest terms of abuse in the jazz-man's vocabulary. Charles Winick attributes the 'cool and detached' feel of be-bop and 'progressive' jazz to the use of heroin amongst musicians (see Winick, 1969).

3 The New York sound grew out of a series of impromptu jam-sessions at Minton's and, subsequently, a number of smaller clubs on 52nd Street (The Onyx, Famous Door, Samoa, Downbeat, Spotlight and Three Deuces) during the mid-1940s. Charlie Parker, Dizzy Gillespie and Thelonius Monk are perhaps the most famous names associated with the Sound and their music supported a whole subterranean culture (dark glasses, berets, heroin, minimal communication with the audience, etc.) (see Russell, 1972).

4 Albert Goldman, *Ladies and Gentlemen, Lenny Bruce*. This book makes essential reading for anyone interested in the cultural background to the beat and hipster styles. Goldman places Bruce firmly within the tradition of contemporary jazz and sees the inspired and largely improvised 'raps' (or 'spritzes') of humourists like Bruce, Lord Buckley and Harry 'The Hipster' Gibson as

'part of the same impatient process of short-circuiting the obvious and capping the conventional'.

5 The equation 'jazz' and 'drugs'/'crime' was soon enshrined in the demonology of the popular press. This led to the usual distortions. For example, Hentoff reports that a general business pianist, arrested and charged with murder in Washington in 1957, was described as a 'jazz pianist' in the tabloid newspapers. The annual convention of beatniks at the Newport Jazz Festival throughout the 50s, like the mod–rocker 'invasions' of British South Coast resorts during the mid-60s, served as a focus for the moral panic.

6 The term 'counter culture' refers to that amalgam of 'alternative' middle-class youth cultures – the hippies, the flower children, the yippies – which grew out of the 60s, and came to prominence during the period 1967–70. As Hall *et al.* (1976a) have noted, the counter culture can be distinguished from the subcultures we have been studying by the explicitly political and ideological forms of its opposition to the dominant culture (political action, coherent philosophies, manifestoes, etc.), by its elaboration of 'alternative' institutions (Underground Press, communes, co-operatives, 'un-careers', etc.), its 'stretching' of the transitional stage beyond the teens, and its blurring of the distinctions, so rigorously maintained in subculture, between work, home, family, school and leisure.

Whereas opposition in subculture is, as we have seen, displaced into symbolic forms of resistance, the revolt of middle-class youth tends to be more articulate, more confident, more directly expressed and is, therefore, as far as we are concerned, more easily 'read'.

7 Jefferson suggests that the immigrants were popularly associated in the ghettos of West London with racketeering and prostitution, and therefore attracted the teds' hostile attentions.

8 See Melly (1972) for an amusing and well-informed account of the British jazz scene in the 50s. Revivalist jazz, skiffle and trad are all comprehensively treated.

9 Linda Nochlin in her book *Realism* similarly characterizes the fin-de-siecle dandy as being obsessed with the small details rather than with large sartorial gestures:

> The dandy's costume, contrary to popular belief, was distinguished by its restraint – colour and textures were subdued . . . restraint was exercised in richness of material and flamboyance was generally avoided, distinction provided by subtle little points of detail or refinement, noticeable mainly to other 'insiders'.

10 John Grant, an 80-year-old former farm-hand recalls how the labourers' traditional deference could conceal a fierce sense of pride which enabled them to magically 'own' the work which, by necessity, they sold for a pittance: 'they . . . worked perfectly because it was their work. It belonged to *them*' (Blythe, 1972).

11 According to Barker and Little (1964), the average mod earned about £11 a week, was either a semi-skilled or more typically an office worker, whereas the average rocker was unskilled and earned rather less. In the absence of an equivalent survey of the teddy boys, we can only infer their class origins and job status from contemporary accounts. None the less, Stan Cohen and Paul Rock, in their study 'The Teddy Boy' and Tony Jefferson in 'The Cultural Responses of the Teds' agree on the teddy boys' low or near-lumpen status.

12 Goldman is here referring to conventional images of the criminal underworld – an exact negation of 'straight' values:

> In that age of universal conformity (America in the 50s), it was believed that there lurked beneath the familiar surfaces of life an anachronistic underworld of ruthlessly appetitive and amoral beings who

achieved heroic intensities through the violence of their rebellion against the middle class norms. (Goldman, 1974)

13 Genet compares criminal slang to the 'language of men among the Caribbes'. He sees both as fundamentally male preserves: '. . . a secondary sexual attribute. It was like the coloured plumage of male birds, like the multi-coloured silk garments which are the prerogatives of the warriors of the tribe. It was a crest and a spurs' (Genet, 1966).

14 'Crazy baldhead' became current as a term of abuse in reggae around 1974–5. It refers literally to those who don't wear 'dreadlocks' but can be used to designate all the 'sinners' who remain tied to Babylon.

15 Carter deplores the current revival of 1940s womens' fashion styles, talks despairingly of 'the iconography of helplessness' and accuses both the designers and those women who wear high heels of 'revisionism at foot level'.

16 The implicit 'threat' to traditional British values is of course most clearly exploited by the National Front. Indeed, Rastafarianism seems to have been identified as a kind of black bacillus by the N.F. For instance, a N.F. poster depicting a black face, framed in dreadlocks 'melting' onto a union jack, interprets the black presence as a literal 'sullying' of British culture.

17 As well as providing a stimulating gloss to Genet's work, Sartre's famous essay (1963) contains many insights into the psychology of subculture in general. Sartre interprets Genet's wilful elevation of crime into art as a truly 'heroic' act of self-transcendence. Born a bastard, adopted by a peasant family and named a thief at the age of nine, Genet systematically contravenes civic, sexual and moral law, aspiring towards the condition of the utterly abject 'which turns out to be next door to

saintliness'. In Genet's own words (1967) '. . . we arouse pity by cultivating the most repulsive of wounds. We became a reproach to your happiness'. As Kate Millett writes in *Sexual Politics* in Genet's 'mortification, both in the flesh and the spirit, lies the victory of the saint'.

18 The punk look was essentially undernourished: emaciation standing as a sign of Refusal. The prose of the fanzines was littered with references to 'fat businessmen' and 'lard-ass capitalists'. Paul Weller of the Jam flatly refused to take the more recent music of Roger Daltrey (lead singer of the Who) seriously because 'you can't play rock 'n roll with a beer-gut' (*New Musical Express*, 7 May 1977). The movement from metaphorical to literal frames of reference seems a crucial part of the process of 'magical resolution' (see pp. 77–8) common to all spectacular subcultures.

19 See Richard Hell, *New Musical Express*, 29 October 1977, on the significance of being rechristened a punk: 'One thing that I wanted to bring back to rock 'n roll was the knowledge that you invent yourself. That's why I changed my name'. Punks in pursuit of an 'immaculate' identity often adopted aliases – Paul Grotesque, Sid Vicious, Johnny Rotten, etc.

20 One punk assured me in October 1977 that punk's only claim to political significance lay in the fact that 'we're like *that* with the blacks', indicating by clasping his hands together that the interests of the two groups were inseparable.

21 Listen for instance to Elvis Costello's 'Watching the Detectives' which has a strong reggae rhythm. Punk dub consists of a series of independently recorded tracks, superimposed one on top of the other without being perfectly synchronized. Without stretching the point too far we could say that dub alienates the listener from the prevailing aesthetic of unobtrusive naturalism (i.e. the polished product). It leaves the studio door open.

22 R & B groups like the Yardbirds, Them, the Animals, the Pretty Things and the Rolling Stones readily acknowledged their black American sources. Jagger frequently claimed to have modelled his celebrated dance routines on the stage act of James Brown. Groups like the Small Faces, the Who, Zoot Money, and Georgie Fame and the Blue Flames – all extremely popular with the mods – did cover versions of soul classics (particularly numbers originally recorded by Bobby Bland, James Brown, Otis Redding and Wilson Picket). See Charlie Gillet's excellent *Sound of the City* for a thorough account of black American music in the 1950s and 1960s.

23 The subcultural styles of these periods in particular were 'scrambled' in the punk ensembles and the lyrics and self-presentation of some of the American punk groups (especially Mink DeVille and Blondie) reiterated in a quite deliberate way the theme of 'crazy mixed-up' adolescence firmly associated with the earlier periods (c.f. the Shangri-Las).

Chapter 5

1 American sociologists and psychologists have tended to lay the stress on adolescence as a period of individualism and transition marked by ritual conflict:

> Although the concepts of 'childish' and 'adult' differ from one culture to another, every culture requires *some* change in the child's habitual ways of thinking, feeling and acting – a change which involves psychic dislocation and therefore constitutes a 'problem' for the individual and the culture. (Kenniston, 1969)

A comparative approach can be illuminating, but it can also serve to obscure important historical and cultural differences. What one can say about youth in general is strictly limited.

2 See Hoggart (1958). The debate about the alleged disintegration of working-class consciousness was conducted on the Left most notably by E. P. Thompson and Professor C. Wright Mills, and was extended by Westergaard, Lockwood and Parkin. This exchange had centred on whether or not a number of developments since the War – the rise of consumerism, and the prospect of the affluent worker, the diminution of primary poverty, the erosion of the traditional community, the provision of educational ladders, the role of the trade unions, the influence of the mass media, etc. – had served permanently to 'bourgeoisify' the working class (see, in particular, Thompson, 1960 and Westergaard, 1972). For an excellent summary and critique of the arguments put forward by Lockwood and Parkin, see Brook and Finn (1977).

The strange mixture of bomb-sites and relative affluence, of old habits and new appetites, was captured in the novels of the 'angry young men' of the 1950s, in particular: John Braine, *Room at the Top* (Allen Lane, 1957); Stan Barstow, *A Kind of Loving* (Penguin, 1962); and Alan Sillitoe, *Saturday Night and Sunday Morning* (Signet, 1970).

3 During the period 1945–50 it was estimated that the average real wage of teenagers increased at twice the adult rate (see Abrams, 1959).

4 Both Downes' study of corner-boy culture in Stepney and Poplar, and Willmott's survey of adolescent options in Bethnal Green gave the lie to the myth of the classless teenager. Downes saw the 'delinquent solution' as a way for working class youth to achieve the ends of 'teenage culture' without having legitimate access to the means. Willmott stressed the local character of East End youth culture: leisure time and money were still spent on the 'manor' rather than in the newly opened boutiques and discotheques of London's West End.

5 Mayhew (1851) and Archer (1865) were among the first to attempt a detailed description of the criminal underworld in London's East End 'rookeries' (see Chesney, 1972 for a highly readable summary of their work).

6 Charles Dickens, *Oliver Twist* (1838)
  Arthur Morrison, *A Child of the Jago* (1896)
  The Hole in the Wall (1902)
  Dickens needs no recommendation. However, the novels of Arthur Morrison are perhaps less familiar. Based on his own childhood experiences in the notorious Jago 'rookery', they provide a fascinating if depressing account of life in a mid-nineteenth-century slum.

7 See Roberts (1976) for a thorough account of the development of P.O. work and the problems it raises: 'PO has never become a complete alternative to positivism in sociology. . . . Instead, it has formed a sort of sociological "subculture" of its own: a more humanistic and "empathetic" enclave within the mainstream'. See also Jock Young (1970), for an analysis of the contradictions inherent in the sociology of deviance.

8 In *Delinquency and Drift* Matza gives his original thesis a slightly different tilt by describing how adolescent boys 'drift' into deviance. The pursuit of subterranean goals and values draws them into deviance and this is further reinforced by the labelling process.

9 Abrams was involved in market research rather than sociology and was interested specifically in opening up a youth market based on the American model. He saw age rather than class as the single most important source of difference in an affluent post-war society: 'Under conditions of general prosperity the social study of society in class terms is less and less illuminating. And its place is taken by differences related to age.'

10 Listen for example to Jonathan Richman's 'Roadrunner' ('I'm in love with the Modern World'). All the

hymns to plastic were no doubt heavily tinged with irony.

11 This seems to be the position which Ros Coward is attacking in 'Class, Culture and the Social Formation':

> This position is one which posits a direct relation in which Marxist theory is put at the service of socialist tendencies which pre-exist any elaboration. In this way, it reduces the pressing and difficult problem of articulation between the theoretical and the political, and the possibility of the mutual determination between these instances.

Coward goes on:

> The work on sub-cultures . . . relies on a conception of history as the progressive unfolding of some inner principle (in this case economic contradiction) . . . it confuses consciousness and political and ideological representations and relies ultimately on a 'belief' that the working-class are the bearers of solution to conflict, that they somehow represent total mastery, the whole person which will be expressed in socialism.

Arguing from a Lacanian position, Coward presses for a displacement away from the study of culture (which she sees as an 'idealist' construct) to an analysis of the constitution of the individual subject in language. (For the reply to this article see *Screen, Autumn 1978, Vol. 18, No. 3.*)

12 Heavy metal is, as the name suggests, a heavily amplified, basic form of rock which relies on the constant repetition of standard guitar riffs. Afficionados can be distinguished by their long hair, denim and 'idiot' dancing (again, the name says it all). Heavy metal has fans amongst the student population, but it also has a large working-class following. It seems to represent a curious blend of hippy aesthetics and football terrace machismo.

13 Stuart Hall (1977), and also John Fiske and John Hartley (1978). The role the media play in shaping and maintaining consent is crucial. Hall argues that 'The media serve, in societies like ours, ceaselessly to perform the critical ideological work of "classifying out the world" within the "discourse of the dominant ideologies".' This is done by the continual drawing and redrawing of the line between 'preferred' and 'excluded' readings, the meaningful and the meaningless, the normal and the deviant. In passing, Hall also defines and makes connections between 'culture', 'ideology' and 'signification'. Obviously a footnote cannot do justice to an argument of such scope and density, and I can only recommend that readers look for themselves.

Chapter 6

1 This was part of a speech made by Dr George Simpson, a Margate magistrate, after the mod–rocker clashes of Whitsun 1964. For sociologists of deviance, this speech has become *the* classic example of rhetorical overkill and deserves quoting in full: 'These long-haired, mentally unstable, petty little hoodlums, these sawdust Caesars who can only find courage like rats, in hunting in packs' (quoted in Cohen, 1972).

2 On 1 December 1976 the Sex Pistols appeared on the Thames twilight programme *Today*. During the course of the interview with Bill Grundy they used the words 'sod', 'bastard' and 'fuck'. The papers carried stories of jammed switchboards, shocked parents, etc. and there were some unusual refinements. The *Daily Mirror* (2 December) contained a story about a lorry driver who had been so incensed by the Sex Pistols' performance that he had kicked in the screen of his colour television: 'I can swear as well as anyone, but I don't want this sort of muck coming into my home at teatime.'

3 The police brought an unsuccessful action for obscenity against the Sex Pistols after their first L.P. 'Never Mind the Bollocks' was released in 1977.

4 On 4 January, 1977 the Sex Pistols caused an incident at Heathrow Airport by spitting and vomiting in front of airline staff. The *Evening News* quoted a check-in desk girl as saying: 'The group are the most revolting people I have ever seen in my life. They were disgusting, sick and obscene.' Two days after this incident was reported in the newspapers, E.M.I. terminated the group's contract.

5 The 1 August 1977 edition of the *Daily Mirror* contained just such an example of dubious editorial concern. Giving 'serious' consideration to the problem of ted–punk violence along the King's Road, the writer makes the obvious comparison with the seaside disturbances of the previous decade: '[The clashes] must not be allowed to grow into the pitched battles like the mods and rockers confrontations at several seaside towns a few years back.' Moral panics can be recycled; even the same events can be recalled in the same prophetic tones to mobilise the same sense of outrage.

6 The characters that stamp products as commodities, and whose establishment is a necessary preliminary to the circulation of commodities, have already acquired the stability of natural, self-understood forms of social life before man seeks to decipher, not their historical character, for in his eyes they are immutable, but their meaning. (Marx, 1970)

7 The definitive study of a moral panic is Cohen's *Folk Devils and Moral Panics*. The mods and rockers were just two of the 'folk devils' – 'the gallery of types that society erects to show its members which roles should be avoided' – which periodically become the centre of a 'moral panic'.

> Societies appear to be subject, every now and then, to periods of moral panic. A condition, episode, person or group of persons emerges to become defined as a threat to societal values and interests; its nature is presented in a stylised and stereotypical fashion by the mass media; the moral barricades are manned by editors, bishops, politicians and other right-thinking people; socially accredited experts pronounce their diagnoses and solutions; ways of coping are evolved or (more often) resorted to; the condition then disappears, submerges or deteriorates and becomes more visible. (Cohen, 1972)

Official reactions to the punk subculture betrayed all the classic symptoms of a moral panic. Concerts were cancelled; clergymen, politicians and pundits unanimously denounced the degeneracy of youth. Among the choicer reactions, Marcus Lipton, the late M.P. for Lambeth North, declared: 'If pop music is going to be used to destroy our established institutions, then it ought to be destroyed first.' Bernard Brook-Partridge, M.P. for Havering-Romford, stormed, 'I think the Sex Pistols are absolutely bloody revolting. I think their whole attitude is calculated to incite people to misbehaviour.... It is a deliberate incitement to anti-social behaviour and conduct' (quoted in *New Musical Express*, 15 July 1977).

8 See also 'Punks have Mothers Too: They tell us a few home truths' in *Woman* (15 April 1978) and 'Punks and Mothers' in *Woman's Own* (15 October 1977). These articles draw editorial comment (a sign of recognition on the part of the staff of the need to reassure the challenged expectations of the reader?). The following anecdote appeared beneath a photograph showing two dancing teddy boys:

> The other day I overheard two elderly ladies, cringing as a gang of alarming looking punks passed them, say

in tones of horror: 'Just imagine what their children will be like'. I'm sure a lot of people must have said exactly the same about the Teddy Boys, like the ones pictured . . . and Mods and Rockers. That made me wonder what had happened to them when the phase passed. I reckon they put away their drape suits or scooters and settled down to respectable, quiet lives, bringing up the kids and desperately hoping they won't won't get involved in any of these terrible Punk goings-on.

9 'The fairy-tale of the artist's creativity is western culture's last superstition. One of Surrealism's first revolutionary acts was to attack this myth . . .' (Max Ernst, 'What is Surrealism?' quoted in Lippard, 1970).

10 'Surrealism is within the compass of every conscious-ness' (surrealist tract quoted in Lippard, 1970). See also Paul Eluard (1933): 'We have passed the period of individual exercises'.

   The solemn and extremely reverential exhibition of Surrealism, mounted at London's Hayward Gallery in 1978 ironically sought to establish the reputation of individual surrealists as artists and was designed to win public recognition of their 'genius'. For a comparison of punk and surrealism, see below the sections entitled 'Style as Bricolage' and 'Revolting Style'. It is fitting that punk should be absorbed into high fashion at the same time as the first major exhibition of Dada and surrealism in Britain was being launched.

11 On 7 December one month before E.M.I. terminated its contract with the Sex Pistols, Sir John Read, the record company's Chairman, made the following state-ment at the annual general meeting:

   Throughout its history as a recording company, E.M.I. has always sought to behave within contem-porary limits of decency and good taste – taking into account not only the traditional rigid conventions of one section of society, but also the increasingly liberal attitudes of other (perhaps larger) sections . . . at any given time . . . What is decent or in good taste compared to the attitudes of, say, 20 or even 10 years ago?

It is against this present-day social background that E.M.I. has to make value judgements about the content of records . . . Sex Pistols is a pop group devoted to a new form of music known as 'punk rock'. It was contracted for recording purposes by E.M.I. . . . in October, 1976 . . . In this context, it must be remembered that the recording industry has signed many pop groups, initially controversial, who have in the fullness of time become wholly acceptable and contributed greatly to the development of modern music . . . E.M.I. should not set itself up as a public censor, but it does seek to encourage restraint. (quoted in Vermorel, 1978)

Despite the eventual loss of face (and some £40,000 paid out to the Pistols when the contract was terminated) E.M.I. and the other record companies tended to shrug off the apparent contradictions involved in signing up groups who openly admitted to a lack of professionalism, musicianship, and commitment to the profit motive. During the Clash's famous performance of 'White Riot' at the Rainbow in 1977 when seats were ripped out and thrown at the stage, the last two rows of the theatre (left, of course, intact) were occupied almost exclusively by record executives and talent scouts: C.B.S. paid for the damage without complaint. There could be no clearer demonstration of the fact that symbolic assaults leave real institutions intact. Nonetheless, the record companies did not have everything their own way. The Sex Pistols received five-figure sums in compensation from both A & M and E.M.I. and when their L.P. (recorded at last by Virgin) finally did reach the shops, it contained a scathing attack on E.M.I. delivered in Rotten's venomous nasal whine:

> You thought that we were faking
> That we were all just money-making
> You don't believe that we're for real
> Or you would lose your cheap appeal.
> Who?
> E.M.I. – E.M.I.
>
> Blind acceptance is a sign
> Of stupid fools who stand in line
> Like E.M.I. – E.M.I. ('E.M.I.', Virgin, 1977)

Chapter 7

1 Although structuralists would agree with John Mepham (1974) that 'social life is structured like a language', there is also a more mainstream tradition of research into social encounters, role-play, etc. which proves overwhelmingly that social interaction (at least in middle-class white America!) is quite firmly governed by a rigid set of rules, codes and conventions (see in particular Goffman, 1971 and 1972).

2 Hall (1977) states: '. . . culture is the accumulated growth of man's power over nature, materialised in the instruments and practice of labour and in the medium of signs, thought, knowledge and language through which it is passed on from generation to generation as man's "second nature"'.

3 The terms 'anarchic' and 'discourse' might seem contradictory: discourse suggests structure. None the less, surrealist aesthetics are now so familiar (though advertising, etc.) as to form the kind of unity (of themes, codes, effects) implied by the term 'discourse'.

4 In his P.O. account of the Saturday night dance in an

industrial town, Mungham (1976) shows how the constricted quality of working-class life is carried over into the ballroom in the form of courtship rituals, masculine paranoia and an atmosphere of sullenly repressed sexuality. He paints a gloomy picture of joyless evenings spent in the desperate pursuit of 'booze and birds' (or 'blokes and a romantic bus-ride home') in a controlled setting where 'spontaneity is regarded by managers and their staff – principally the bouncers – as the potential hand-maiden of rebellion'.

5 BOF = Boring old Fart
   Wimp = 'wet'.

6 Gilbert and George mounted their first exhibition in 1970 when, clad in identical conservative suits, with metallized hands and faces, a glove, a stick and a tape recorder, they won critical acclaim by performing a series of carefully controlled and endlessly repeated movements on a dais while miming to Flanagan and Allen's 'Underneath the Arches'. Other pieces with titles like 'Lost Day' and 'Normal Boredom' have since been performed at a variety of major art galleries throughout the world.

7 Of course, rock music had always threatened to dissolve these categories, and rock performances were popularly associated with all forms of riot and disorder – from the slashing of cinema seats by teddy boys through Beatlemania to the hippy happenings and festivals where freedom was expressed less aggressively in nudity, drug taking and general 'spontaneity'. However punk represented a new departure.

8 The word 'punk', like the black American 'funk' and 'superbad' would seem to form part of that 'special language of fantasy and alienation' which Charles Winick describes (1959), 'in which values are reversed and in which "terrible" is a description of excellence'.

   See also Wolfe (1969) where he describes the 'cruising'

scene in Los Angeles in the mid-60s – a subculture of custom-built cars, sweatshirts and 'high-piled, perfect coiffure' where 'rank' was a term of approval:

> Rank! Rank is just the natural outgrowth of Rotten ... Roth and Schorsch grew up in the Rotten Era of Los Angeles teenagers. The idea was to have a completely rotten attitude towards the adult world, meaning, in the long run, the whole established status structure, the whole system of people organising their lives around a job, fitting into the social structure embracing the whole community. The idea in Rotten was to drop out of conventional status competition into the smaller netherworld of Rotten Teenagers and start one's own league.

Chapter 8

1 Sylvia Harvey *May 68 and Film Culture* (British Film Institute, 1978). This is an extremely lucid introduction to the notoriously difficult work of the 'second wave' semioticians (much of which has yet to be translated into English). Harvey traces the development of radical film theory in France from the appropriation of Russian formalism by the journals *Cahiers* and *Cinétique* in the early 70s to the beginnings of 'a science of the signifier' as developed by the *Tel Quel* group in Paris.

2 The film journal *Screen* has largely been responsible for opening up this debate in Britain. See MacCabe (1975) for another representative critique of realism.

3 Brecht intended that his 'epic theatre' should let the audience 'in' on the 'secret' of its own construction through the celebrated 'alienation techniques' which have the effect of distancing the spectator from the spectacle and, theoretically at least, making him or her reflect on the social relations depicted in the play and on

his or her *position* on (rather than 'in') the text. By preventing audience identification with character, and by
avoiding plot continuity, resolution, etc., epic theatre is
supposed to jar the audience into the recognition that
'reality is alterable' (see *Brecht on Theatre* (Willett, 1978)).
Brecht's preoccupation with formal techniques and their
role in the politicization of theatre has proved extremely
influential in the formation of the new film theory (see
Harvey, 1978).

4 As part of his attempt to break down the traditional
unity of narrative, Eisenstein based his theory of mon-
tage (the juxtaposition of shots in film) on the principle
of 'collision' rather than 'linkage' (see Harvey, 1978,
p. 65).

5 I can only refer the reader to A. White's critique (1977)
for an explication of Kristeva's use of terms like the
'symbolic' and of the dialectic between unity and process, the 'symbolic' and the 'semiotic' which forms the
thematic core of her work:

> The symbolic is . . . that major part of language which
> names and relates things, it is that unity of semantic
> and syntactic competence which allows communica-
> tion and rationality to appear. Kristeva has thus divided
> language into two vast realms, the *semiotic* – sound,
> rhythm and movement anterior to sense and linked
> closely to the impulses (Triebe) – and the *symbolic* –
> the semantico-syntactic function of language necessary
> to all rational communication about the world. The
> latter, the *symbolic*, usually 'takes charge of' the semio-
> tic and binds it into syntax and phonemes, but it can
> only do so on the basis of the sounds and movements
> presented to it by the semiotic. The dialectic of the
> two parts of language form the *mise en scene* of Kris-
> teva's description of poetics, subjectivity and revolu-
> tion.

(See also G. Nowell-Smith's introduction to 'Signifying Practice and Mode of Production' in the *Edinburgh '76 Magazine*, no. 1.)

6   The setting in place, or constituting of a system of signs requires the identity of a speaking subject in a social institution which the subject recognises as the support of its identity. The traversing of the system takes place when the speaking subject is put in process and cuts across, at an angle as it were, the social institutions in which it had previously recognised itself. It thus coincides with the moment of social rupture, renovation and revolution. (Kristeva, 1976)

Again, Kristeva is specifically concerned with positing a notion of the *subject in process* against the traditional conception of the single, unified subject, and she uses the terms 'significance', 'symbolic', 'semiotic' and 'imaginary' in the context of Jacques Lacan's theory of psychoanalysis. Her definition of 'signifying practice' none the less still holds when transplanted to the quite different context of the analysis of style in subculture.

7   'Who knows if we are not somehow preparing ourselves to escape the principle of identity?' (A. Breton, Preface to the 1920 Exhibition of Max Ernst).

8   See, for instance, *Melody Maker*, 30 July 1977 and *Evening Standard*, 5 July 1977. The teddy boys interviewed typically complained of the punks' lack of stylistic integrity and accused them of trying to be 'clever'.

9   '. . . it is the *way in which* the semiotic relates to and disfigures the symbolic, as well as the *way in which* the symbolic reasserts its unifying control of the semiotic, which gives us the basis of subjectivity as a process' (White, 1977). Similarly, it is the way in which subordinate groups relate to and disfigure the symbolic order which gives us the basis of subculture as a mode of resistance.

Chapter 9

1 In taking this quotation out of context, I am no doubt doing a disservice to Nuttall, who is far less guilty than many of his contemporaries of misrepresenting style in subculture. Despite the dated title, *Bomb Culture* is still one of the most readable and authoritative 'appreciations' of the post-war youth 'explosion'.

2 Scholte (1970). Here Scholte contrasts the epistemological premises of structural anthropology against the Anglo-American school which operates empiricist and functionalist models.

3 The hostility between punks and latter-day skinheads was a refinement which occurred too recently to gain a mention in the descriptive section. By October 1977 the skinheads had emerged as a separate faction inside the punk subculture, together with their own musical heroes (Skrewdriver, Sham 69, reggae performers) and their more straightforwardly lumpen personae. The hostility seemed to be rather one-way, and punks, constricted by their bondage-gear, were no match for the more fight-oriented skins.

Conclusion

1 It turned out to be life. In June 1970, Jackson was transferred to San Quentin where, one year later at the age of 29, he was shot dead by prison guards, 'trying to escape'.

2 In Genet's prison hierarchy, the 'jerk' is the lowest of the low. Even the 'chickens' can if they wish refuse a 'mac', a pimp or a 'big shot'; the 'jerk' is freely available at any time to anybody.

3 Genet, 1963. The master-servant dialectic of mutual degradation is thoroughly explored in Genet's plays. The Maids have been colonized to such an extent that

they have become monstrous – the 'seamy side of their Masters', their 'unwholesome exhalations', so lost in self-loathing that they see themselves as each other's 'bad smell'. See also K. Millett on Genet in *Sexual Politics*.

4 In his Introduction to *Our Lady of the Flowers*, Sartre describes Genet's language as a 'dream of words . . . (it) suffers from deep lesions, it is stolen, faked, poeticised'.

5 Contrary to this thesis, there is evidence that cultures of resistance actually sometimes serve to reinforce rather than erode existing social structures. In his book, *Learning to Labour*, Paul Willis sets out to explain 'how working class kids get working class jobs' and comes to the conclusion that the 'counter-culture of the school' helps to reproduce the manual labour force by stressing the traditional masculine values of the working-class community (e.g. manual as opposed to mental work, physical strength and wit against scholarship, etc.).

6 Jean-Paul Sartre, from an interview in 'New York Review of Books' (26 March 1970)

> . . . I believe that a man can always make something of what is made of him. This is the limit I would today accord to freedom: the small movement which makes of a totally conditioned social being someone who does not render back completely what his conditioning has given him. Which makes of Genet a poet when he had been rigorously conditioned to be a thief.

7 In *Generation X*, Hamblett and Deverson quote a 16-year-old mod from South London: 'You'd really hate an adult to understand you. That's the only thing you've got over them – the fact that you can mystify and worry them.'

8 See Sontag (1970) for a diagnosis of the peculiar dilem-

ma in which the anthropologist (urban or otherwise) is caught: '. . . the man who submits himself to the exotic to confirm his own inner alienation ends by aiming to vanquish his subject by translating it into a purely formal code'. For Sontag, the 'metier of the adventurer as a spiritual vocation' is a specifically twentieth-century phenomenon deriving from the work of 'wanderers' like Conrad, T. E. Lawrence, St-Exupery, Montherlant and Malraux. Although the student of deviance engaged in P.O. work could hardly be called an 'adventurer', there are certain parallels. Like the anthropologist proper, camping out in an alien culture, in Sontag's words, 'he can never feel himself "at home" anywhere; he will always be, psychologically speaking, an amputee.'

BIBLIOGRAPHY

Abrams, M. (1959), *The Teenage Consumer*, London Press Exchange.

Althusser, L. (1969), *For Marx*, Allen Lane.

—— (1971a), *Lenin and Philosophy and Other Essays*, New Left Books.

—— (1971b), 'Ideology and Ideological State Apparatuses', in *Lenin and Philosophy and Other Essays*, New Left Books.

Althusser, L. and Balibar, E. (1968), *Reading Capital*, New Left Books.

Archer, T. (1865), *The Pauper, the Thief and the Convict*.

Arnold, M. (1868), *Culture and Anarchy*.

Barker, P. and Little, A. (1964), 'The Margate Offenders: A Survey', *New Society*, 30 July, reprinted in T. Raison (ed.), *Youth in New Society*, Hart-Davis, 1966.

Barstow, S. (1962), *A Kind of Loving*, Penguin.

Barthes, R. (1971), 'The Rhetoric of the Image', *W.P.C.S.* 1, University of Birmingham, retranslated in S. Heath (ed.), *Image, Music, Text*, Fontana, 1977.

—— (1972), *Mythologies*, Paladin.

—— (1977a), 'The Third Meaning', in S. Heath (ed.), *Image, Music, Text*, Fontana.

—— (1977b), 'Writers, Intellectuals, Teachers', in S. Heath (ed.), *Image, Music, Text*, Fontana.

Becker, H. S. (ed.) (1964), *The Other Side: Perspectives on Deviance*, Free Press.

Bennett, T. (1979), *Formalism and Marxism*, Methuen.

Berger, J. (1967), *A Fortunate Man*, Penguin.

Bigsby, C. W. E. (ed.) (1976), *Approaches to Popular Culture*, Arnold.

Blackburn, R. (ed.) (1972), *Ideology and the Social Sciences*, Fontana.

Blythe, R. (1972), *Akenfield: Portrait of an English Village*, Penguin.

Braine, J. (1957), *Room at the Top*, Penguin.

Breton, A. (1924), 'The First Surrealist Manifesto', in R. Seaver and H. Lane (eds), *Manifestoes of Surrealism*, University of Michigan Press, 1972.

—— (1929), 'The Second Surrealist Manifesto', in R. Seaver and H. Lane (eds), *Manifestoes of Surrealism*, University of Michigan Press, 1972.

—— (1936), 'Crisis of the Object', in L. Lippard (ed.), *Surrealists on Art*, Spectrum, 1970.

—— (1937), 'Introduction to an Anthology of Surrealist Poetry', in L. Lippard (ed.), *Surrealists on Art*, Spectrum, 1970.

Brook, E. and Finn, D. (1977), 'Working Class Images of Society and Community Studies', *W.P.C.S.* 10, University of Birmingham.

Burniston, S. and Weedon, C. (1977), 'Ideology, Subjectivity and the Artistic Text', *W.P.C.S.* 10, University of Birmingham.

Burroughs, W. (1969), *The Wild Boys*, Caldar & Boyers.

Burrows, D. and Lapides, F. (eds) (1969), *Alienation: A Casebook*, Crowell.

Carmago-Heck, M. de (1977), 'The Ideological Dimensions of Media Messages', unpublished M.A. thesis, University of Birmingham.

Carter, A. (1976), 'The Message in the Spiked Heel', *Spare Rib*, 16 September.

Chesney, K. (1970), *The Victorian Underworld*, Penguin.

Chambers, I. (1976), 'A Strategy for Living', in S. Hall *et al.* (eds), *Resistance Through Rituals*, Hutchinson.

Clarke, J. (1976a), 'The Skinheads and the Magical Recovery of Working Class Community', in S. Hall *et al.* (eds), *Resistance Through Rituals*, Hutchinson.

——— (1976b), 'Style', in S. Hall *et al.* (eds), *Resistance Through Rituals*, Hutchinson.

Clarke, J. and Jefferson, T. (1976) 'Working Class Youth Cultures' in G. Mungham and C. Pearson (eds), *Working Class Youth Culture*, Routledge & Kegan Paul.

Cohen, A. (1955), *Delinquent Boys: The Culture of the Gang*, Free Press.

Cohen, P. (1972a), 'Sub-cultural Conflict and Working Class Community', *W.P.C.S.* 2, University of Birmingham.

Cohen, S. (1972b), *Folk Devils and Moral Panics*, MacGibbon & Kee.

Cohen, S. and Rock, P. (1970), 'The Teddy Boy', in V. Bogdanor and R. Skidelsky (eds). *The Age of Affluence*, Macmillan.

Corrigan, P. (1976), 'Doing Nothing', in S. Hall *et al.* (eds), *Resistance Through Rituals*, Hutchinson.

Coward, R. (1977), 'Class, "Culture" and the Social Formation', *Screen*, vol. 18, no. 1.

Culler, J. (1976), *Saussure*, Fontana.

Curran, J., Gurevitch, M., Deverson, J. and Woollacott, J. (eds) (1977), *Mass Communication and Society*, Arnold.

Douglas, M. (1967), *Purity and Danger*, Penguin.

Downes, D. (1966), *The Delinquent Solution*, Routledge & Kegan Paul.

Eco, U. (1972), 'Towards a Semiotic Enquiry into the Television Message', *W.P.C.S.* 3, University of Birmingham.

——— (1973), 'Social Life as a Sign System', in D. Robey

(ed.), *Structuralism: The Wolfson College Lectures 1972*, Cape.

Eliot, T. S. (1963), *Notes Towards a Definition of Culture*, Faber.

—— (1959), *Four Quartets*, Faber.

Eluard, P. (1933), *Food for Vision*, Editions Galliard.

Ernst, M. (1948), *Beyond Painting and Other Writing by the Artist and His Friends*, ed. B. Karpel, Sculz.

Fanon, F. (1967), *Black Skins, White Masks*, Grove.

Fineston, H. (1964), 'Cats Kicks and Colour', in H. S. Becker (ed.), *The Other Side: Perspectives on Deviance*, Free Press.

Fiske, J. and Hartley, J. (1978), *Reading Television*, Methuen.

Geertz, C. (1964), 'Ideology as a Cultural System', in D. E. Apter (ed.), *Ideology and Discontent*, Free Press.

Genet, J. (1963), *The Maids*, Faber.

—— (1966a), *Our Lady of the Flowers*, Panther.

—— (1966b), *The Blacks*, Faber.

—— (1967), *The Thief's Journal*, Penguin.

—— (1971), Introduction to *Soledad Brother: The Prison Letters of George Jackson*, Penguin.

Gillet, C. (1970), *The Sound of the City*, Sphere.

Godelier, M. (1970), 'Structure and Contradiction in "Capital" ', in M. Lane (ed.), *Structuralism: A Reader*, Cape.

Goffman, E. (1971), *The Presentation of Self in Everyday Life*, Penguin.

—— (1972), *Relations in Public*, Penguin.

Goldman, A. (1974), *Ladies and Gentlemen, Lenny Bruce*, Panther.

Goodman, P. (1968), 'Objective Values', in C. Cooper (ed.), *The Dialectics of Liberation*, Penguin.

Hall, S. (1974), 'Deviancy, Politics and the Media', in P. Rock and M. McIntosh (eds), *Deviance and Social Control*, Tavistock.

—— (1975), 'Africa is Alive and Well and Living in the

Diaspora', unpublished paper given at UNESCO conference.

—— (1977), 'Culture, the Media and the "Ideological Effect"', in J. Curran *et al.* (eds), *Mass Communication and Society*, Arnold.

Hall, S., Clarke, J., Jefferson, T. and Roberts, B. (eds) (1976a), *Resistance Through Rituals*, Hutchinson.

—— (1976b), 'Subculture, Culture and Class', in S. Hall *et al.* (eds), *Resistance Through Rituals*, Hutchinson.

Hamblett, C. and Deverson, J. (1964), *Generation X*, Tandem.

Harvey, S. (1978), *May '68 and Film Culture*, British Film Institute.

Hawkes, T. (1977), *Structuralism and Semiotics*, Methuen.

Hannerz, U. (1969), *Soulside: An Inquiry into Ghetto Culture and Community*, Columbia Press.

Heath, S. (ed.) (1977), *Image, Music, Text*, Fontana.

Hebdige, D. (1976), 'Reggae, Rastas and Rudies', in S. Hall *et al.* (eds), *Resistance Through Rituals*, Hutchinson.

Hell, R. (1977), interview in *New Musical Express*, 29 October.

Hentoff, N. (1964), *The Jazz Life*, Panther.

Hiro, D. (1972), *Black British, White British*, Penguin.

Hoggart, R. (1958), *The Uses of Literacy*, Penguin.

—— (1966), 'Literature and Society', *American Scholar*, Spring.

Ingham, R. (ed.) (1977), *Football Hooliganism*, Inter-action Imprint.

Jefferson, T. (1976a), 'The Cultural Meaning of the Teds', in S. Hall *et al.* (eds), *Resistance Through Rituals*, Hutchinson.

—— (1976b), 'Troubled Youth, Troubling World', in G. Mungham and G. Pearson (eds), *Working Class Youth Culture*, Routledge & Kegan Paul, 1976.

Jones, Le-Roi (1975), *Blues People*, MacGibbon & Kee.

Kenniston, K. (1969), 'Alienation and the Decline of Utopia', in D. Burrows and F. Lapides (eds), *Alienation: A Casebook*, Crowell.

Kerouac, J. (1958), *On the Road*, Deutsch.

Kristeva, J. (1974), *La Revolution du langage poetique*, Seuil.

—— (1975), 'The Speaking Subject and Poetical Language', paper presented at University of Cambridge.

—— (1976), 'Signifying Practice and Mode of Production', *Edinburgh '76 Magazine*, no. 1.

Kidel, M. (1977), 'Trenchtown', *New Statesman*, 8 July.

Lackner, H. and Matias, D. (1972), 'John Ford's *Young Mister Lincoln*', *Screen*, vol. 13, no. 3, originally published in *Cahiers*, no. 233, 1970.

Laing, D. (1969), *The Sound of Our Time*, Sheen & Ward.

Lane, M. (ed.) (1970), *Structuralism: A Reader*, Cape.

Lautréamont, Comte de (1970), *Chants du Maldoror*, Alison & Busby.

Lefebvre, H. (1971), *Everyday Life in the Modern World*, Allen Lane.

Levi-Strauss, C. (1966), *The Savage Mind*, Weidenfeld & Nicolson.

—— (1969), *The Elementary Structures of Kinship*, Eyre & Spottiswood.

Lippard, L. (ed.) (1970), *Surrealists on Art*, Spectrum.

MacCabe, C. (1974), 'Notes on Realism', *Screen*, vol. 15, no. 2.

—— (1975), 'Theory and Film: Principles of film and pleasure', *Screen*, vol. 17, no. 3.

Mailer, N. (1968), 'The White Negro', in *Advertisements for Myself*, Panther.

—— (1974), 'The Faith of Graffiti', *Esquire*, May.

Marx, K. (1951), 'The Eighteenth Brumaire', in *Marx and Engels Selected Works*, vol. 1, Lawrence & Wishart.

—— (1970), *Capital*, Lawrence & Wishart.

Marx, K. and Engels, F. (1970), *The German Ideology*, Lawrence & Wishart.

Masson, A. (1945), 'A Crisis of the Imaginary', *Horizon*, vol. 12, no. 67, July.

Matza, D. (1964), *Delinquency and Drift*, Wiley.

Matza, D. and Sykes, G. (1961), 'Juvenile Delinquency and Subterranean Values', *American Sociological Review*, no. 26.

Mayhew, H. *et al.* (1851), *London Labour and the London Poor*.

Melly, G. (1970), *Owning Up*, Penguin.

—— (1972), *Revolt into Style*, Penguin.

Mepham, J. (1972), 'The Structualist Sciences and Philosophy', in D. Robey (ed.), *Structuralism: The Wolfson College Lectures 1972*, Cape, 1973.

Mepham, J. (1974), 'The Theory of Ideology in "Capital" ', *W.P.C.S.*, no. 6, University of Birmingham.

Miller, W. (1958), 'Lower-Class Culture as a Generating Milieu of Gang Delinquency', *Journal of Social Issues*, 15.

Millett, K. (1972), *Sexual Politics*, Sphere.

Mungham, G. (1976), 'Youth in Pursuit of Itself', in G. Mungham and G. Pearson (eds), *Working Class Youth Culture*, Routledge & Kegan Paul.

Mungham, G. and Pearson, G. (eds) (1976), *Working Class Youth Culture*, Routledge & Kegan Paul.

Nochlin, I. (1976), *Realism*, Penguin.

Nowell-Smith, G. (1976), Introduction to J. Kristeva, 'Signifying Practice and Mode of Production', *Edinburgh '76 Magazine*, no. 1.

Nuttall, J. (1969), *Bomb Culture*, Paladin.

Picconne, P. (1969), 'From Youth Culture to Political Praxis', *Radical America*, 15 November.

Raison, T. (ed.) (1966), *Youth in New Society*, Hart-Davis.

Reverdy, P. (1918), *Nord-Sud*.

Roberts, B. (1976), 'Naturalistic Research into Subcultures and Deviance', in S. Hall *et al.* (eds), *Resistance Through Rituals*, Hutchinson.

Robey, D. (ed.) (1973), *Structuralism: The Wolfson College Lectures 1972*, Cape.

Russell, R. (1973), *Bird Lives!*, Quartet.

Sartre, J. -P. (1964), *Saint Genet, Actor and Martyr*, Braziller.

—— (1966), Introduction to J. Genet, *Our Lady of the Flowers*, Panther.

—— (1970), Interview in *New York Book Review*, 26 March.

Saussure, F. de (1974), *Course in General Linguistics*, Fontana.

Seaver, R. and Lane, H. (eds) (1972), *Manifestoes of Surrealism*, University of Michigan Press.

Scholte, B. (1970), 'Epistemic Paradigms', in E. Nelson Hayes and T. Hayes (eds), *Levi-Strauss: The Anthropologist as Hero*, MIT Press.

Shattuck, R. (1969), *The Banquet Years: Origins of the Avant-Garde in France 1885–World War One*, Cape.

Sillitoe, A. (1970), *Saturday Night and Sunday Morning*, Penguin.

Sontag, S. (1970), 'The Anthropologist as Hero', in E. Nelson Hayes and T. Hayes (eds), *Levi-Strauss: The Anthropologist as Hero*, MIT Press.

Taylor, I. and Wall, D. (1976), 'Beyond the Skinheads', in G. Mungham and G. Pearson (eds), *Working Class Youth Culture*, Routledge & Kegan Paul.

Thompson, E. P. (1960), 'The Long Revolution', *New Left Review*, nos 9 and 10.

Thrasher, F. M. (1927), *The Gang*, University of Chicago Press.

Tolson, A. (1977), 'The Language of Fatalism', *W.P.C.S.*, no. 9, University of Birmingham.

Vermorel, F. and Vermorel, J. (1978), *The Sex Pistols*, Tandem.

Volosinov, V. N. (1973), *Marxism and the Philosophy of Language*, Seminar Press.

Westergaard, J. H. (1972), 'The Myth of Classlessness', in R. Blackburn (ed.), *Ideology and the Social Sciences*, Fontana.

White, A. (1977), 'L'eclatement du sujet: The Theoretical Work of Julia Kristeva', paper available from University of Birmingham.

Whyte, W. F. (1955), *Street Corner Society*, Chicago University Press.

Williams, R. (1960), *Border Country*, Penguin.

—— (1961), *Culture and Society*, Penguin.

—— (1965), *The Long Revolution*, Penguin.

—— (1976), *Keywords*, Fontana.

Willet, J. (trans.) (1977), *Brecht on Theatre*, Methuen.

Willis, P. (1972), 'The Motorbike Within a Subcultural Group', *W.P.C.S.* no. 2, University of Birmingham.

—— (1977), *Learning to Labour*, Saxon House.

—— (1978), *Profane Culture*, Routledge & Kegan Paul.

Willmott, P. (1969), *Adolescent Boys in East London*, Penguin.

Winick, C. (1959), 'The Uses of Drugs by Jazz Musicians', *Social Problems*, vol. 7, no. 3, Winter.

Wolfe, T. (1969), *The Pump House Gang*, Bantam.

—— (1966), *The Kandy-Kolored Tangerine Flake Streamline Baby*, Cape.

Young, J. (1970), 'The Zoo-Keepers of Deviance', *Catalyst* 5.

—— (1971), *The Drug Takers*, Paladin.

SUGGESTED FURTHER READING

GIVEN the spectacular nature of the subject, it is hardly surprising that a vast literature has grown up around subculture. For the same reason, it is inevitable that the quality of the available commentaries should be uneven. On the one hand, many of the 'popular' accounts are superficial and poorly researched, whilst, on the other, serious 'respectable' works are all too often couched in an inappropriately solemn prose. The following selection attempts to salvage the best from both the academic and journalistic traditions. *Resistance Through Rituals* (Hall *et al.*, 1976) and *Working Class Youth Culture* (Mungham and Pearson, 1976) should require no further recommendation as I have referred to them throughout. They are both essential reading. This List should be regarded as supplementary to the text references and Bibliography.

Subcultural theory

Howard Becker's *The Outsiders: Studies in the Sociology of Deviance* (Free Press, Glencoe, 1963) is an acknowledged 'classic' in the field of deviancy studies and still stands as one of the best examples of the transactional method in which the construction of deviant groups is interpreted as the result of a dynamic process whereby those in power define the limits of acceptable and unacceptable behaviour through *labelling* (e.g. marijhuana smoker = lazy, long-haired, potentially violent malcontent, etc.). The theoretical exposition is integrated into a fascinating account of the 'Jazz Life' during the 1940s and 1950s (Becker was himself a professional jazz musician for some years).

Also written out of the tradition of transactional analysis, *The Manufacture of the News. Deviance, Social Problems and the Mass Media* (S. Cohen and J. Young, (eds), Constable, 1973) examines, in the editors' words, 'the conceptions of deviance and social problems revealed in the mass media and the implicit view of society behind such conceptions'. The labelling process is here described in terms of the media's *selection* and *presentation* of news on various groups (gays, alcoholics, the mentally ill, political deviants, drug-takers, etc.). In a final section, Cohen and Young consider the *effects* of that coverage upon the groups themselves. See also *Images of Deviance* (S. Cohen (ed.), Penguin, 1971) and *Politics and Deviance* (I. Taylor and L. Taylor, Penguin, 1973), collections of papers given at the National Deviancy Conference, and *Deviance and Social Control* (P. Rock and M. McKintosh, (eds), Tavistock, 1973).

Finally, *Policing the Crisis* (S. Hall, T. Jefferson, J. Clarke, and B. Roberts, MacMillan, 1978) combines theoretical and empirical approaches to study the growth of the British mugging 'scare' of the early 1970s. The authors follow the course of a particularly sensational case from the arrest to the eventual conviction of three Birmingham youths, and examine the judgement in the light of the Law and Order campaign launched during the period. In the process, they trace the origin of the term 'mugging' and show how a combination of circumstances – the economic crisis, the breakdown of consensus, changes in black identity, etc. – conspired to imbue the alleged increase in street-violence with an ominous significance.

Youth culture

See Whyte (1955) and Thrasher (1927) for early examples of the 'naturalistic' research of the Chicago school. B. Roberts' 'Naturalistic Research into Subcultures and Deviance' (in Hall *et al.* 1976a) is an extremely competent survey and critique of the development and theoretical implications of research based on participant observation. For the debate on the sources and meaning of the value system and focal concerns of American street-gangs, see A. Cohen (1955), W. Miller (1958) and D. Matza and G. Sykes (1961). D. Matza (1964) uses a transactional model to explain the young offender's 'drift' into a deviant 'career'. P. Marsh and A. Campbell bring the picture up to date in two articles on recent gangland activity in the United States: 'The youth gangs of New York and Chicago go into business' (*New Society*, 12 October 1978), and 'The Sex Boys on their own turf' (*New Society*, 19 October 1978). The first questions the dominant assumption that gangland violence in New York declined in the 1960s after the 'classic' West Side Story period and examines the way in which the assumed resurgence of such violence in recent years is being used as a metaphor for America's decline. The second article, based on interviews with members of the Sex Boys street gang explores the focal concerns of modern New York gangs and shows how the importance of 'rep' (reputation) and 'heart' (courage; English equivalent: 'bottle') remains undiminished.

Though it is important to distinguish between the delinquent *gang* (small, with a specific local recruitment, a local set of loyalties, and a strong commitment to 'machismo', subterranean values and illegal activities) and the *subculture* which is altogether broader, looser, less strictly defined by class and regional membership and less literally involved in law-breaking, there are obvious connections (e.g. gangs like the Quinton Boys, a group of Midlands skinheads, can exist within subcultures). Moreover, the two terms are virtually synonomous in the popular mythology. Unfortunately, the confusion that follows from this association (about class, violence, etc.) has all too often been reproduced in academic work because, as we have seen, the analysis of subculture grew in large part directly *out of* the study of delinquent street gangs.

See D. Downes (1966) and P. Willmott (1969) for empirically based studies of British working-class youth culture in the late 1950's and early 1960's. See also P. Willis (1978a and b) for participant observation studies of hippies, motor bike boys and cultures of resistance in school. P. Cohen (1972) reconstructs the post-war history of the East End of London by interpreting the succession of working-class youth styles as a series of creative responses to changing conditions. He introduces the notion that style represents a 'magical resolution' of experienced contradictions.

Nik Cohn's *Awopbopaloobop Alopbamboom* (Paladin, 1970) together with Melly's *Revolt into Style* (1972) and Nuttall's *Bomb Culture* (1969) still contain the most stimulating and evocative resumées of the first two decades of rock music and the British youth cultures which grew up round it. All Tom Wolfe's work, though confined with a few notable exceptions to the American scene, is well worth reading. By adding empathy to observation, Wolfe manages to catch the unique flavour of each subculture – both its exclusive 'feel' and the meaning of the rituals, argot and value system through which it is defined. See in addition to Wolfe (1966, 1969), *Radical Chic and Mau-Mauing the Flak-Catchers* (Bantam, 1971), an amusing study of the obsessive cultivation by radical intellectuals of deviant acquaintances and outlawed causes. Also *The Electric Kool-Aid Acid Test* (Bantam, 1969), in which Wolfe follows the trail of Ken Kesey and the Pranksters – a group of perpetually hallucinating anarchists – in a 'magic bus' across the America of the hippie era. Written in the same spirit, *Fear and Loathing in Las Vegas* (Hunter S. Thompson, Paladin, 1974), though not specifically concerned with subculture, is a brilliantly subversive extension of the Meaningful American Journey (the Quest for the West) undertaken by the author and his lawyer under the influence of a whole range of drugs. Thompson's also produced a participant observation account of an American motor-cycle gang entitled *Hell's Angels* (Penguin, 1967) which ends, convincingly enough, with Thompson himself being severely 'stomped' by his 'subjects'. For a brief look at the meaning of British subcultural style, see J. Nuttall's 'Techniques of Separation' in *Anatomy of Pop* (Tony Cash (ed.), B.B.C. publication, 1970).

Music

Simon Frith's *The Sociology of Rock* (Constable, 1976) provides the first detailed analysis of the rock music business from the discovery of young talent through the packaging, refinement and promotion of a musical style to the actual production and distribution of the musical product. *The Story of Pop* (Phoenix Press, 1975) and *All Our Loving* (T. Palmer, Weidenfeld & Nicholson, 1976) are accessibly written and visually stimulating 'coffee table books', though Palmer supplies the more idiosyncratic and in places questionable account. R. Mabey's *The Pop Process* (Hutchinson 1969) is a 'critical exploration' of the pop music world of the 1960's though the emphasis on the 'value' of the lyrics may seem a little dated now. See also D. Laing, 'The Decline and Fall of British Rhythm and Blues' in the *Age of Rock* (Eisen (ed.), Random House, 1969) and 'Musical Developments in Pop' in Cash (1970). *The Encyclopedia of Rock* (Laing, D and Hardy, P. (eds)) is a useful reference book which contains information on all the major performers, producers and record companies from 1955–1975.

For black American soul, see C. Gillett (1969), P. Garland, *The Sound of Soul* (Chicago 1969) and 'A Whiter

Shade of Black' in Eisen (ed.) 1969. Also, L. Jones, *Black Music* (Apollo, 1968).

Beats and hipsters

See Bibliography for A. Goldman (1974), R. Russell (1972), H. Finestone (1964), L. Jones (1975), N. Hentoff (1964), N. Mailer (1968), J. Kerouac (1958), H. Becker (1963, 1964). In addition, H. Gans' *The Urban Villagers* (Glencoe, 1963) is a study of the American bohemian scene in the late 1950s, and N. Polsky, *Hustlers, Beats and Others* (Penguin, 1971) as well as containing a fascinating piece of research on pool room hustlers, includes an essay on the role of marijhuana in the world of drifters, beats and drop-outs. For the jazz background, see I. Gitler's *Jazz Masters of the Forties* (MacMillan, 1966), B. Green's *The Reluctant Art* (Lancer Books, 1967) and A. Goldman's *Freakshow* (Atheneum, 1971). For the literary background, see William Burrough's *Junkie* and *The Naked Lunch* (Corgi, 1970), and Jack Kerouac's *The Dharma Bums* (Panther, 1972). Also Ann Charters' excellent biography *Kerouac* (Picador, 1978).

Teddy boys

See Jefferson (1976). Jefferson sees the teddy boy style as an expression of both the reality and the aspirations of the group. T. Fyvel's *The Insecure Offenders* (Chatto and Windus, 1963) contains a contemporary response to the teddy boy phenomenon. H. Parker's *View from the Boys* (David and Charles, 1974) is an account of the 1953 Clapham Common Murder which did much to establish the teddy boys' repution for violence. See also S. Cohen and P. Rock (1970), a study of reactions in the media to the teddy boy style, and J. Sandilands 'Whatever happened to the Teddy Boys?' (in *Daily Telegraph Magazine*, 29 November 1968).

Mods

See Bibliography for D. Laing (1969), S. Cohen (1972), D. Hamblett and J. Deverson (1964). D. Hebdige's 'The Style of the Mods' gives a reading of mod style which stresses both the mods' symbolic subversion and fetishization of commodities. Gary Herman's study of *The Who* (Studio Vista, 1971) is one of the first attempts to relate the style and success of a pop group to a particular subculture. See also, K. Hatton's 'The Mods' in the *Sunday Times Colour Magazine*, 2 August 1964, a photographic feature with quotations from interviewed mods. Since writing the book, there has been a mod revival which attracted the attention of the press when the Who staged a re-enactment of the mod-rocker confrontations for their film *Quadrophenia* (see *Melody Maker*, 24 October 1978).

Skinheads

J. Clarke (1976) interprets the skinhead style as an attempt to resurrect the fading chauvanisms of traditional working-class culture against the inroads of consumerism and embourgeoisment. *The Paint House: Words from an East End Gang* (S. Daniel and P. McGuire (eds), 1972) contains transcripts of conversations with a group of London skinheads and builds up a depressingly authentic picture of lives trapped between school, home and unskilled work. See also P. Fowler's 'Skins Rule' in *Rock File* (C. Gillett (ed.), New English Library, 1970).

Hippies

A mass of literature was produced in and around the counter-culture during the late 1960s, but two books stand out as representative of the hippie experience: taken together, R. Neville's *Playpower* (Paladin, 1971) and T. Roszack's *The*

Making of the Counter Culture (Faber, 1971) give a reasonably full account of the movement in Great Britain and the U.S. See also J. Young (1971) and 'The Hippies: An Essay in the Politics of Leisure' in I. Taylor and L. Taylor (eds), (1973). Further reading should include J. Rubin's *Do It! Scenarios of the Revolution*, an indictment of 'Amerika' and a statement of anarchic intent. Rubin was a leading spokesman for the yippies (a politically militant off-shoot of the hippies which owed a certain amount to the Paris-based Situationists). The transition from hippie to yippie is best explained by Rubin himself: 'Yippies are hippies who've been hit on the head by policemen'.

Reggae, Rastas and rudies

For a full account of the early history of the Rastafarian movement in Jamaica and a detailed exposition of the movement's aims and beliefs, see M. G. Smith, R. Angier and R. Nettleford, *The Ras Tafarian Movement in Kingston, Jamaica* (Institute for Social and Economic Research, U.C.W.I., Kingston, Jamaica). Rex Nettleford's *Mirror, Mirror* (William Collins & Sangster, Jamaica, 1970) and L. E. Barrett's *The Rastafarians* (Heinemann, 1977) place the movement in the context of a centuries-old tradition of resistance to colonization in the Caribbean. J. Owens' *Dread: The Rastafarians* (Sangster, 1976) which consists of edited conversations with Rastafarians testifies to the complexity and depth of Rasta religious convictions and to the persuasive use of figurative language made by individual brethren. For an analysis of reggae in Jamaica, see *Reggae Bloodlines* (Davis, S. and Simon, P., Ancher 1977).

For black youth in Britain, see D. Hiro (1972) and D. Hebdige (1976). Also C. McGlashan, 'Reggae, reggae, reggae' in *Sunday Times Colour Magazine* (4 February 1973) contains interviews with reggae musicians and sound-system men and a description of a Saturday night 'blues' party. V.

Hines' *Black Youth and the Survival Game in Britain* (Zulu Press, 1973) deals as the title suggests with the day-to-day experience of disadvantage. See also Hall *et al.* (1978). Articles on reggae and the cultural background in both Britain and Jamaica appear regularly in the music press. See in particular, *Black Echoes*, *Black Music*, *New Musical Express* and *Sounds*.

Punk

It is still too early to provide any comprehensive or confident evaluation of existing accounts of the punk subculture. At the moment of writing, only two studies seem of more than ephemeral interest. F. and J. Vermorel (1978) have provided an adequate account of the early history of the Sex Pistols. T. Parker and J. Burchill's *The Boy Looked at Johnny* (Pluto Press, 1978) claims to be an 'obituary to rock 'n roll'. Written in an exaggerated 'scandal-sheet' style, the book is an exposé of rock's dubious ethics and dwells in particular upon the disjunction between punk's aspirations and achievements. The authors write with the acidic fervour of the newly disillusioned but the book does give a genuine 'insider' account of the punk subculture. See also any edition of the *New Musical Express* from November 1976 to June 1978.

INDEX

Figures in **bold** type indicate a main reference.